The Historical Chronicles of Elinor Sturgeon and the Last Human Colony.

Volume I

R.T. Kilgore

ISBN: 978-0-9657113-7-1

Library of Congress Control Number: 2019933919

Living Springs Publishers

WWW.LivingSpringsPublishers.com

Cover design and illustrations by Ken Bastard

ACKNOWLEDGEMENTS

I want to start by thanking my father, for inspiring my love of both reading and writing at a young age, and for reading every draft I have ever written. You are the smartest man I know and you can still make me laugh harder than anyone else. I will forever be in your debt and I will spend my entire life striving to reach your capacity for everything literary.

I would like to thank a dear friend and confidant, James Kelly. You were there during the beginnings of this novel and were nothing but positive through all the cringing and eye rolling. Your friendship and endless motivation truly made this book happen.

Lastly, I would like to thank Living Springs Publishers for taking a shot on a new author. I know science fiction is not your usual genre, and that makes your feedback and expertise even more appreciated.

Contents

The Historical Chronicles of Elinor Sturgeon and the Last Human Colony.

Volume I

Dictated by:

Commander Elinor Sturgeon

(no number or classification assigned)

In its original Parian.

Translations available upon request.

Dictation begins: Turn 96 of Rotation 51,080,905,672.

Location: Sharron, Qualittia

ELINOR

1.

Reminiscent of multi-colored mountains, five figures loomed over my half-conscious human form as my mind floated out of stasis and into reality. My body had somehow found its way onto an alien vessel while my thoughts continued to wander around space.

Approximately three fractions must pass for a human to come fully out of stasis, and during those three fractions the mind is aware, but the body is helpless. As the kaleidoscope of colors, that I would later learn were members of the species Par and a part of the 27th squadron in the Kara Warrior forces, picked me up from where I lay in my stasis chamber and carried me into a very white, echoing space. I could hear them speaking with each other, but I didn't understand a word at that time. Although, the sounds reminded me of the ancient romance languages of my species.

I could sense I was moving but the alabaster labyrinth made it hard to tell how far. The frosted walls closed in on me, and I was placed on what I took to be an iceberg while a pink cloud hovered overhead. I felt calm and tried to reach out and touch the cloud but my brain did not send the request to my hand.

The pink blur, which would soon be introduced as Urralysttical 8655, shifted me onto my side. I have a hazy memory of wondering what would come next. Then suddenly, without warning, the most intense pain I have ever experienced surged its way up my spine and wedged itself firmly in the middle of my skull. Everything went black.

On the bright side I eventually woke up, but I suppose there was no real suspense in that regard since we're at the beginning of the adventure not the end. The pain eventually subsided but there was a sense of growth and searching left behind, like I was trying to remember a character's name from a book I read as a child. I attempted to put words into place and organize my thoughts, but fuzzy mumbles kept pushing their way to the center of my cognitive process.

I was alone. The room was sterile, begging to be smudged. I remained where I was and let my eyes do the searching. I realized I was in no way constrained and so I sat up to get a better view of the bleached void. I heard someone approaching and immediately became aware of my nakedness. I was in the process of curling myself into a ball, covering all the necessary parts, as one of the large colorful blobs entered the room. There was no door, just an opening that lead into an identically white hallway. The purple blob that had carried me from my stasis pod now stood two steps in front of me as a clearly formed Par male.

The creature leering at me was massive and ugly, but not as alien as I would have liked to think. This was the male that would soon introduce himself to me as Lesshoosha 7866, Les for short. His muscular form lined up with mine perfectly except for the fact that he was twice my size. My head reached right below his shoulders, and his body was at least double my width. His appendages added to the same number as mine; as did his facial features. The biggest difference between our physical appearances was the deep purple hue to his thick, calloused skin. Also, as you know, human's noses protrude from their face and we only have one set of nostrils. We greatly suffered for this in the thin air of Qualittia.

Les wore tight black booty shorts, which would soon become my common attire, as it was for all Kara Warriors. The sharp spikes sprinkled along his head, arms, and spine are another characteristic unique to Kara warriors. His large black eyes with clear eyelids locked onto mine in a neverending stare. His lips were by far the most appealing part of his face. Full and wide but at this moment contorted into a sneer as he eyeballed me from across the room.

He started trying to communicate with me but all I could make out were a bunch of "Whooshes" and "Glunks." It wasn't like he was making noises I had never heard before, but they certainly didn't add up to equal any language I understood at the time. I translated my confusion as best I could into a facial expression, which was immediately comprehended, and he fell silent. At that time, I was not aware of the LiquiParian flowing through my cerebral cortex; working on embedding the Par language into my memory and allowing me to communicate with ease.

He approached me and I unintentionally shrunk away. I didn't fear him nearly as much as I should have at that time, but his size alone caused me to cower. I could tell scaring me had not been his motivation as he set a cup of red liquid down on the table before backing out of the room.

He didn't restrain me or close the opening when he left. I could leave whenever I wanted. I considered the possibility that I was still floating safely in my pod having a stasis dream, but if that is true this has been a very long dream indeed, since I am now an old woman with a head full of memories. At the time of my discovery, I had spent half of my short life working as a Searcher, but never once thought I would find anything on my search missions. I just enjoyed the solitude.

I contemplated running, trying to fight my way back to my ship, but then realized that running would go against everything I had been trained for. I had finally fulfilled the purpose of every mission I had ever gone on. Of course, I didn't move. I continued sitting in the white room silently over-thinking everything and freaking myself out while my new acquaintance did the same thing in his room about fifty steps away.

***

Suddenly there were two of them. Urral and Les entered the room. Urral did not frighten me the way his purple companion had. I don't know why since he was a good two hands taller than his purple friend, which put my head at his chest, but he was much skinnier than the purple lug and didn't have nearly as much intensity pulsing through his body. He was as calming as his color tone and even gave me a small smile as he entered the room behind his scowling leader.

Urral started talking in their foreign language as he slowly approached me. He stretched out his hands between us as if I was a dangerous animal, he was unsure of. I didn't move in case the big one was there to pounce on me for misbehaving. Pinkie gave me a concerned look and walked to the wall on the far side of the room. He lifted his hand and swiped it vertically down the wall. The wall to the right of me faded to reveal a view of space outside. For a moment I was afraid he had opened an airlock to dispose of me, but no change in air pressure occurred so I maintained my silence. He then returned to my side and was holding a clear, square screen. He lifted his transparent screen up to align with my eyes and started moving it closer and further away as if to get the picture he was looking at into focus. They continued to talk, ignoring me except for the occasional awkward glance. I persevered in my ignorant silence and waited for them to leave so I could go back to focusing on what I assumed was going to be my inevitable death.

Soon they came to some conclusion, and I wondered if they shared my sense of hopelessness about our situation. They looked at each other and then me, paused for a brief moment like two adults deciding what to do with a child neither of them wanted, and then big and purple approached the wall in front of me where an indentation had formed. Cylindrical containers appeared, and he pulled a jar from the shelf and placed it in the middle of the indented space. A beam of clear liquid poured into the cylinder, which once full was set down beside the untouched jar of red liquid that rested beside my thigh. He slide both closer to me. Tall and pink was over by the wall as well, and soon returned with a large, fluffy pink blanket. I had few expectations at this point, but a fluffy pink blanket was not even on my radar. He crossed the room and draped the blanket around my shoulders and before I could properly contain myself a snorting laugh pushed past my lips.

"Pinkie are you serious? Your sense of color scheme surprises me beyond your terrifying bodies." I don't know how or why my brain decided to speak up at that specific moment, but I think my shock was wearing off.

The only answer I got in return was my new acquaintances backing away from me as if I had just promised to blow up their ship with the explosives I had hidden in my fallopian tubes.

These two males, that would eventually become my close companions, stared at me from the exit and I glared back as best I could. I had no idea what was going on in their heads at that moment, and I didn't care. I wanted to be back in my pod, alone with my own mundane thoughts.

That's the absurdity of the human condition. We crave change our whole lives; searching for something new and different that will set us apart from the everyday bullshit we have convinced ourselves is somehow not really living, but how can that be true? The boring bits of life take up far more time than the thrilling adventures. The boring bits make us who we are.

Yet, we cling to the fleeting moments, blow them up in our minds, and build a reality around them. All the while ignoring the vast majority of our lives as we daydream about being unique flowers that get to live happily ever after. None of us wants to admit that we are all equally significant in our meaninglessness.

I was no more destined for something grand than any other random humanoid. I was just in the right place at the right time. There is no karmic, kismet destiny that chose me for this individualized mission. I'm not unique and deserving of an adventure. I'm a human female like the billions of other human females that have lived and died before me. I want to be normal and happy but have always dreamed of being looked at as truly sui generis, but after my individualized moment revealed itself to me I was terrified and wanted nothing to do with it. Despite the pounding in my heart I certainly didn't feel like I was finally living. I felt like I was waiting to die, but I guess that's what we're all doing all the time.

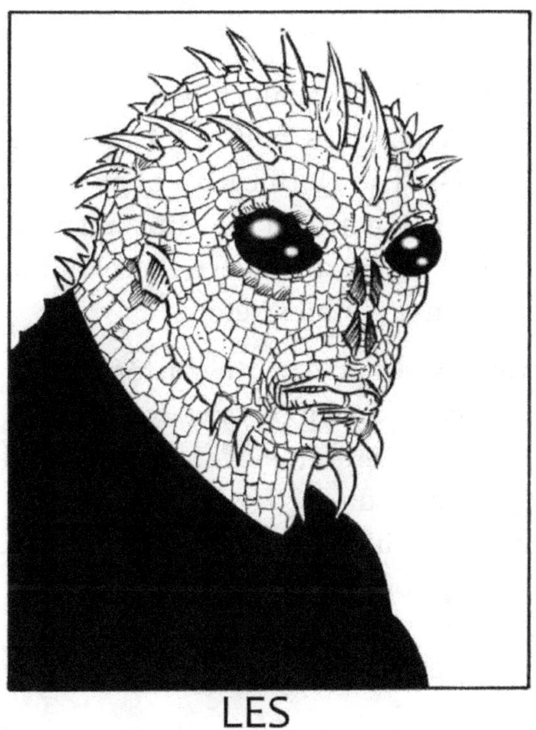

LES

2.

Yesterday's recording is my first memory of the Par, but I'm going to back up just a tad more to where it all began for me.

I am Commander Elinor Sturgeon: Destroyer of Galaxies, and so the best equipped to record the history of the Vokkna War. This is not a history of humanity as a whole. Better to let that nonsense fade into oblivion. This chronicle will be a record of how we came into contact with the Par, and our place in the Vokkna Wars.

Humans, and my actions specifically, changed nothing and saved no lives. We merely perpetuated the very cycle of death we fought against. If you learn only one thing from these chronicles let it be this; one species by itself is meaningless. The glorification of my species is a lie, and without the assistance of the Hurran and Par warriors we would have failed in every aspect of the fight; like we have so many times before.

I suppose I was asked to create this historical document as a sort of homage to myself, but what is history besides the documentation of someone's pride? What is a hero without a villain? The Vokkna are the central characters here. Villains get things done! Heroes just sit around waiting for a foe to vanquish. Main characters are commonly unimaginative in their approach and jump to unnecessary conclusions far too often.

Despite all of this, I will comply with the govenor's wishes and record these historical logs. I have little left to do with my time in my old age, and the history would most certainly be lost without my recollections. I will begin about 75 rotations back when I was young and foolish, and not yet aware of the Par's existence.

***

I was locked in stasis, hurtling through space in a small orb of a ship with nothing but my thoughts for company. No need for a physical description at this point. I'm sure you can find any number of pictures of me in the historical logs.

My official position among the humans was Searcher, and the many years I spent in this position enabled me to conclude that the human mind is an unfathomably boring conduit of information. Once a human has been forced to spend an excessive amount of time with their own thoughts for company it becomes painfully clear that we have very little to say, even to ourselves.

I was in my forty-eighth year of life; half asleep and contemplating the inner workings of my foggy young mind as I floated unknowingly toward a pivotal discovery, and I had come to the conclusion that I no longer had anything unique to think about.

I lay out in semiconscious stasis and wondered if there was going to be any flour, an ancient grain, left on Kepler by the time I got back. I hadn't had a pancake in the five years I had been off planet and was craving something fluffy, gooey, and unnaturally sweet. Humans ate synthetic food imitation while out searching but I was usually able to get my hands on good solid grub when back on planet.

When I set out on my Searcher mission there had been one functioning green house and three functioning duplicators left, but over five hundred mouths to feed. Kepler hadn't had real meat transported to planet in over fifty years, and since Kepler was unfit for mammalian life this was the only way to supply fresh animal flesh. The animals on planet could not reproduce in the atmosphere and had been duplicated so many times--who knew what they were made of anymore. The last terraforming tractor had been dismantled for parts and energy the week before I left. I didn't know if I would find anyone alive let alone the ingredients needed to make the fluffy pastry I so desired.

My upbringing was like any average Kepler native--home schooling by artificial intelligence, long bouts of seclusion punctuated by small moments of human interaction, and then a job assignment upon becoming sixteen. My formative years were spent in isolation and I grew to prefer solitude to forced interaction. My brother, Judas Sturgeon, was born eight years after me, and five years after Earth was declared dead. Judas' life was a consequence of my parents' attempts to stop hating each other, a complete accident, and the ultimate cause of my mother's death. Her body had been primped and pulled, and surgically made unfit for childbirth. The few nurses in training were not prepared for the task of cutting my brother from my mother's tiny form and ended up flaying her in the process.

By that time most people were more worried about what had happened on Earth and if we were officially the last of the colonies, but my parents had been raised to ignore the pain of the populace, plus they had shit-tons of money so what the hell did they care about bringing another pair of lungs into existence. I was born into a wealthy governing family and after Earth failed, everyone located in the colonies began to starve or suffocate but my family maintained normality by hiding away in their ivory tower.

When they came for my father I was ready for them. My brother, myself, and our caretaker Ming; yes, the very same Ming Lee that fought beside me in the Vokkna

Wars, but she was a gangly 19 year old girl at this time. We were the only people in the house other than my father, and when the cries came from the door we knew they had come to kill him. I stood in the entry way with the only blade I could find and waited for the mob to break down the door to our compartment. Judas, small even for an eight year old, clung to Ming in the corner of the front room. I knew my father would die that day and was fully aware that he deserved to die for misuse of the colony and its funds, but I refused to allow them to kill him without a fight. I was able to slice the throats of the first two men through the battered doorway before Ming disarmed me and pulled me into the corner with her. I was spared purely because of her cries for mercy. My father, John T. Sturgeon, died in a pathetic heap at my feet and I did not cry for him.

I got to keep my job as a Searcher even though I had yet to find any sign of life in the surrounding solar systems, and by the time I set out on what would be my final Searcher mission there was only enough fuel left for one more trip past Andromeda. But of course, something happened, or else this wouldn't be a very interesting chronicle.

3.

I woke up to Les' formidable presence. As soon as he saw my eyes open he started talking in his strange language again, but this time there was a completely different outcome. His foreign words fluttered through my ears, hit my frontal lobe, and were somehow matched up with their literal and figurative equivalent in my brain. I understood him.

"Wait, what?" Was all I could manage to get out as I lifted myself onto my elbows, maintaining a grip on the pink blanket. The creature's body became rigid. I responded in English but we both knew I had comprehended him and he remained silent as I tried to work out the translation process in my head. Ok brain, we need to ask him what the fuck is going on so just let me say the globidie goop that will equal that. The words were miraculously easy for my mouth to form.

"What the fuck is going on?" The language still sounded like random noises to my ears, but the big guy's eyes widened and he stepped forward.

"It's amazing that both our languages have a vulgar word for such a pleasurable act, and that such a visually appealing creature, a female, would feel comfortable using language only appropriate for males." He seemed to grow in size as he approached and a creepy smile stretched across his face. He showed off his wide, blunt teeth as he added, "I'm glad your system has assimilated the serum. There is much we should talk about." I was still contemplating his previous sentence when he spoke the second. I needed to focus. My brain needed time to translate but as the words became clear I was finding myself offended. Who was this guy, and why did he feel like he could get so close to me?

"Yes," I spoke this slowly in the new language I would soon know as Parian. "Why did you do this? Why am I here?"

As they came out I realized these were not the questions that really mattered. I needed to stop focusing on me and start focusing on the fact that I had just found what I had been searching for since I was sixteen.

I added quickly, "We are… we are extremely similar. Is your home world near and able to inhabit creatures of my specification?" Yes, that was a much better question. We stared at each other for a couple seconds. I didn't like the way he looked at me, but that was a problem to be addressed at a different time.

"My species and yours are, as you have stated, very similar. You are of the same class as I. The Par have been searching for life forms since we first entered the environment outside of our own planet, and you are the fourth we have found, the third intelligent, and the second in classification vertebrate. We have both made a grand discovery here. In response to your third question, my home planet is about two leaps from here and it would be able to sustain a life form such as yours. Are you the last of your kind?"

By the end of his statement he was right on top of me.

I tightened my grip on the pink material wrapped around my torso and gave him a look intended to convey that I did not like him so close to me.

He backed up but only slightly.

"I'm not the last of my species but I was scanning for planets that can sustain my kind of life form." I took a deep breath in an attempt to organize my thoughts. "How is it I can understand you?"

His big lips spread into a smile. I must have asked the right question. "We have injected you with LiqParian. We are the Par. The serum has assimilated with the section of your brain that creates language. I believe yours is located in the front part of your brain." He paused and glanced around the room like there would be someone there to correct his explanation. "We are en route to the coordinates logged into your ship. We detect 71 life forms but there is no way your species could have evolved there. I do not understand why you chose to inhabit that planet." He looked at me in an inquisitive way. I think he was finally waiting for me to respond instead of just staring at me.

"Well, yes, it wasn't our original home planet. It was more of a business venture that didn't really work out. That's why I was out scanning." I took some deep breaths. I was getting ahead of myself. "So how far out are we? We have to be a couple weeks from there. Are we all going into stasis?" I started searching the small room for signs of a pod, which was more of an excuse to break eye contact with the big creep than in real hopes of finding what I was looking for.

"Our technology far surpasses that on your ship. We will use the Zorb to power our leap and will be entering your planet's orbit within 12 hours." He was very proud of this fact. "Zorb?" I arched my eyebrow knowing he was just waiting for an opportunity to continue my education.

"Follow me. I will show you our main bay, and the rest of the ship. I can tell from your ship that you will need to be taught how to survive and function in our society." He began moving to the exit and I started to go after him until I was reminded of my lack of clothing. "Wait, do you have something I can put on? I'd even take the short shorts you're wearing." I pointed at his tiny black shorts, and then was struck with how easy my new language had become. I wasn't even thinking about translating anymore, and I'm pretty sure my taunting tone was getting across. The lack of language barrier made our encounter nearly common place. I kept forgetting I was talking to an alien in a strange language.

"These are our basic uniform designed for comfort, durability, and freedom of movement." He glanced down to where I was pointing and actually looked self-conscious for a moment, but just a moment. "There is no need for you to cover yourself more than you are now. I do not understand why you feel the need to cover any part of your body. Your formation is pleasingly similar to my own." He took a step towards me and I shot my right hand out with my palm facing him. I knew I didn't look intimidating but he stopped so I kept it up.

"Well, I want to cover up and I'm not going anywhere

until you give me something to cover up with other then this thing." My arm then swung around to bring his attention to the bright pink blanket and gave him the bitchiest look I could muster. "If you want me to walk around comfortably I'm going to need real clothes."

His hand went up to stroke the spikes that lined his chin and when he turned to face the wall, I noticed the thick spikes made a line from the top of his skull all the way down his spine. I wondered how similar he and I would look if our skin was removed. As I studied him, he was messing around with what I was beginning to realize was storage. He waved his hand along the right side of the wall and a drawer slid open. I could see stacks of black fabric I assumed were shorts like those that currently clung to the large form I was examining.

He pulled out a pair and brought them to me. "They should fit. Philex is made to take the form of whatever body it is worn by."

The big guy made no move to turn around and continued to keep his eyes fixed on my body. I was about to give him a lecture about manners and respect when I realized, "I don't know your name." I laid the shorts on the table beside me and tightened my grip on the blanket. "I'm Elinor Lee Sturgeon." I threw him off with that. He stepped back and looked around the room again as if he would receive a clue about his own name from the white walls.

"I am Lesshoosha 7866 V. You may address me as Les." He puffed himself out and I assumed I was supposed to be impressed. "It is very rude for a woman to ask the name of a man. In the future you will await permission to become formal with a male, but it is likely our species will have many conflicting customs. Please dress yourself so that we may begin the tour." He turned and began to leave but there was no way I was going to let that go without saying anything.

I slid the shorts on before he turned around, and he was right, they fit snuggly around my hips as if they had been made for me. I was now standing and I crossed the blanket over my breasts. "That is a ridiculous custom. Especially since it appears that Par men are not aware that an introduction should be done at the beginning of a conversation and not in the middle of it."

He was unaffected by my irritated behavior, but he did stop to turn and acknowledge my words. "It is a custom of my people. I understand you do not know our ways and so will allow your rudeness to go unpunished. Soon you will learn how to behave properly." He took a couple steps toward me and once again I was engulfed in his mass. "Please follow me."

I was about to do as I was told, but then remembered something Les had said earlier. "Wait, you said you detected seventy life forms on Kepler?" He was mostly out of the room when I said, "My planet."

"We detected seventy-one healthy life forms on the planet. We also found it to be a disturbingly low number." I thought I heard pity in his voice. I had mixed feelings about this. "Please, allow me to show you my ship and introduce you to my crew. You will feel better once you know more about your surroundings, and then we can discuss our plans for your species." He reached out as if he was about to touch my shoulder and I moved to put more space between us.

I made my way back to the wall and pulled out another pair of shorts. I turned my back to Les and tried to rip the seam so I could wear the bottom as a top. Nothing happened. They barely even stretched out. I could feel Les behind me, "Do you have any tops, or could you rip the crotch of these for me?" I held the black cloth out and he stared at me completely confused.

"Why are you so intent on covering yourself? Have I not made it clear that I wish you to remain as you are?" He took them from me and made a move to toss them back in the drawer. I placed my hand on his forearm and said, "This is one of my customs and I will be much more comfortable meeting your crew if I am covered with something more substantial than a pink blanket." My hand was still on his arm, and as I met his eyes for a moment he begrudgingly turned toward the wall and waved his hand again. A shelf slid out and another drawer opened but this one held what appeared to be an assortment of metal tools. Les grabbed a silver rod about the length of my finger, pressed one end, which caused the other to glow bright blue, and then dragged the lighted end across the crotch of the shorts. "This tool cuts Philex and only Philex." He looked up from his work, smiled at me, and ran the light across my hand. I jumped back with a yelp but looked down to find my skin intact.

"Don't! What the hell?" I snatched the newly split shorts from his hands and backed away from him, but I could not stop the smile from spreading across my face."I knew you would be safe." He returned my smile as he put the cutting device away and pushed in the drawers and shelf. While his back was to me I pulled the recently altered shorts over my shoulders. The material clung to my body and made a strange shape because the cut out crotch left extra material hanging along my back, but it was actually comfortable and form fitting.

I decided to push forward with the I'm-not-terrified-out-of-my-fucking-mind act and said, "Ok, show me this ship and crew of yours."

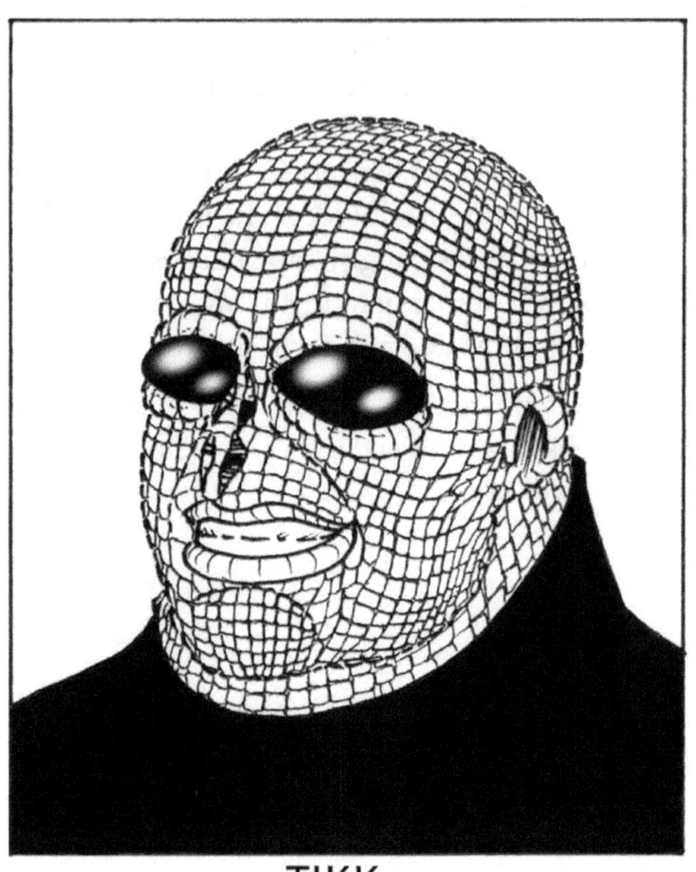

TIKK

4.

I met the sparse crew as Les led me through endless white rooms. We found Runnucclta 6554 V, lanky and crimson red, as he attempted to make the dining hall presentable. I was told to call him Runn, because all Par shorten their official names in casual settings to speed up conversation. I made the massive mistake of introducing myself to Runn, which resulted in him recoiling from my outstretched hand.

"Do not attempt to practice any of your customs with the Par," was all Les said before taking my arm and leading me out of the room.

Then we disturbed the bright pink Urral, as he worked busily in the medical section of the ship. I did not attempt to broach the subject of names with Urral, or the orange hued Inncassatis 8974 V, who we ran into on our way to the control deck. Wide and aqua blue, Bryyluccny 3487 V, nearly ran me over as he came careening out of a side room, but Les caught him with his shoulder; forcing him back into the unknown room all before I was aware anything was happening. I heard an apology trailing after us and Les proceed forward without a second glance.

Shurrantyluk 78865 V was the color of midnight with a personality to match. I wanted his approval the moment I caught sight of his rigid frame. Lyttlyack 57992 V towered over me and I could not help but giggle to myself about the irony that only I could understand. Yurrhallana 43526 V stood beside the massive Lyttl and his red body, that was at least two heads higher than my own, appeared tiny in comparison to Lyttl's mountainous yellow form.

We walked in on Fyddsalat 70652 V, Wynnishon 29976 V, and Cykkliptoo 647789 V tossing differently colored spheres into the air in the midst of some kind of game. They came to a halt as I poked my head into the padded, ivory room. I hopped on the buoyant floor and Les made the introductions. Of the three Par I was captivated by Cykk, who was a dull grey in color. He was still covered in the long spines, but his skin had no bright color, and I could not help but stare.

“I wear my poverty like a badge.” Was the statement he made to me as he caught my eye, but Les grunted and pulled me towards the exit before I could respond.

“This is Tikknnerlack 5998 V, Tikk, he is the ship's Time Engineer and one of the best on Qualittia. He is the one that will make it possible to arrive at your planet so swiftly." Les said as we made it to the main bay of the ship.

Tikk was shorter than Les but he was still about seven centimeters taller than me. He was wide and bright green. Tikk, like Urral, had not spikes on his body. I awkwardly smiled at my new acquaintance and pondered what it was they expected me to do in the moment.

All I could think of was what I wasn't allowed to do, so I could only muster, "Time Engineer?" and a slight tilt of the head. I officially sounded as clueless as I was.

What I would categorize as a laugh burst from Tikk's mouth. He smiled and said, "The name is not accurate, and was formed out of a joke. Of course, we cannot create time.” He shifted from foot to foot and glanced at Les as if asking for permission to speak. “Space and light on the other hand, those are things we can control. We can manipulate. That is what I do. I manipulate space so that it takes us less time to get to where we want to go. I believe that is where the name came from. The Kara soldiers didn't understand what we did but they knew we saved them time and so they came up with the idea for the name. I always preferred the formal Space Organizer." We all stared at each other in silence for a while after that. I had not heard any of the other crew members say more than a couple of words to Les. This new male, that was as comfortable in my presence as I was uncomfortable in his, intrigued me. He did not stare at me the way the rest of them did and for that I was instantly drawn to him.

"How do you do it?" I knew the question was vague and stupid the moment I asked but I wanted to elongate the time I had with this new and somewhat friendly Par. I could feel Les' black-hole eyes pulling me in. I stepped closer to Tikk and said, "I mean, could you explain how it is you manipulate space. Do you kind of fold it?" I opened my hands and brought my fingers together to mimic two parts of space folding together to touch. "My people had been theorizing on how to do that for centuries, but we never really got it right, so we just focused on going faster."

"The Par's main concern in our search for ways to leap vast distances was the form of energy that kind of technology would require. The Zorb can run on any energy source." Tikk was not looking at me like I was a small child or an idiot. I liked him more and more. "As I am sure you know, space is continually expanding. One day it will stop and start contracting, but for now it is malleable and indistinct, and so with the right amount of energy we can shift space into the shape we prefer. Space wants to be moved, it is looking for direction and so I simply give it what it wants. It is all rather exciting, if you are a fan of physics." Tikk glanced at Les and I could feel him seeking approval.

"I find it fascinating." I spoke as I moved so I was between the two of them, showing Les the back of my head. "I'm far from a scientist but I'd be greatly appreciative of a briefing. What does a Zorb leap measure?"

"Let's start with the basics." Tikk said. "The device is located right over here. I believe visual is always the best way to learn." He turned around and began to lead me to the right side of the large, circular room.

The room was bare which allowed the massive window opposite the entrance to monopolize my attention. The only lights on the ship came from the floor. Small orbs every five meters or so shot up tiny beams of white light. My first encounter with the emptiness of a Par ship was flabbergasting, but I now find little need to clutter a room with excess.

I remember the sudden need to use the toilet smack me across the bladder. I pushed the urge to pee to the back of my head and concentrated on Tikk; who was now indicating an area along the wall. As we approached I noticed a small ball of garbage pulsating over a beam of blue light.

"This?" I pointed at the tiny spherical object and tried not to sound as disenchanted as I felt.

Tikk laughed, which put me at ease. Tikk's laugh is a

deep baritone that sounds more like grunting and gurgling but the corners of his mouth stretched towards his jet black eyes as his body shook with joy in a similar fashion to my brother, which brought me great comfort. "When spoken of in that way, the Zorb does not seem very significant. I would like to have been there for your tour, Les. I am sure she made your grand ship into quite a disappointment." I was reminded that Les was standing behind me as the two males caught each other's eye. I turned to see that Les was not humored by my actions the way Tikk was.

"Yes, she is a vocal female, and does not feel the need to subdue her opinions." Les shifted back and forth and took a deep breath a little too close to my neck for comfort. "She will learn our customs." He shifted away as we all pretended not to be uncomfortable.

"I don't mean to belittle it or anything. It's just amazing that something so tiny powers your whole ship. How?" I refocused on Tikk. I hoped Les would get bored and go away.

"Do you see these openings on the back wall?" Tikk indicated the area on the wall behind the Zorb and I became aware of two holes spitting out debry into the ball of trash. "One is hooked up to all the waste receptacles around the ship, and one is connected to our personal waste facilities. The Zorb will consume anything." As he spoke random objects of different color and texture came flying out to the two circles and were immediately consumed by the Zorb. The Par had turned a pile of garbage into a black hole. The Zorb would expand and combust as the objects entered its atmosphere and quickly were consumed.

Tikk continued as gooey waste particles flicked through the air and disappeared. "We could program it to consume anything, even living organisms, and it would, but we realized in the beginning that you cannot program a Zorb to only consume dead flesh. If we put our genetic material on the menu the Zorb won't differentiate between alive and dead. It could consume this entire ship and all of us before I had the chance to change its programing, and so we maintain a specialized menu for the Zorb's consumption." He smiled at my terrified expression. "I promise you are safe." He waved his hand around the grey ball and nothing happened, but when an object from one of the holes came bursting out from wherever in the ship it came from the Zorb sprang into action. "The Zorb then transfers the matter it consumes into kinetic energy, and we harvest that energy to power the ship." Tikk gave me a few moments to digest all of this.

"When will we be ready?" Les spoke up and once again I was reminded how close he liked to stand to me.

"No more than eight fractions, Innc found a recently collapsed star, and we are sending a Zorb out to harvest it now. That should give us enough energy and then some for the trip home." Tikk caught my questioning gaze and continued, "We have a total of five Zorbs on board. We had more but they can get worn down over time. The platform in the middle of the room is where our link to the engine is located."

He nodded towards the middle of the expansive room and I noticed a slight shadow in the area he indicated. If it had not been pointed out I would never have noticed it.

"When… no, an explanation will not suffice. Here…" He grabbed the Zorb off the shelf and walked to the back of the room. Another Zorb emerged as he tossed the original toward the darkened area. When it reached the center of the room, a beam of sapphire light froze the Zorb in place. The Zorb, inside the funnel of light, exploded into millions of tiny pieces but remained inside the force field.

Tikk faced me and said, "Now the ship is prepared to fold space and make a jump, but this Zorb only has enough energy stored to take us a short way and so it would be pointless to jump only half way home, not knowing if where we land will have proper fuel." He reached out and waved his hand up the side of the scattered remnants, which collapsed back into a small ball that he caught in mid-fall. "And there you have it; Zorb travel for beginners." I decided then and there that I was going to be friends with this Tikk fellow.

"I have a not completely unrelated question to ask." I shifted away from them. "Do you have a toilet, or a place where I could… release some personal waste?" I was trying to be polite.

"Les, you didn't show her where the facilities are?" Tikk tossed the Zorb back towards the wall where it disappeared.

This was my first experience with Par emotion. Les' eyes flashed pitch-black-blue and crystal white as he said, "I did show her. She said, 'Fine, on to the next random room,' and walked out. She does not focus when I speak." The beauty of Les' sparkling eyes was shaded by my expanding bladder.

"All the rooms on this thing look exactly the same," I shouted louder than I should have. "How are you supposed to know which is which? You have to indicate where we are with words; not just awkward stares." I had pushed and jabbed at each of them numerous times during my speech. I was not disgusted by their strangeness or scared by their size. Our ability to share a common language had given me confidence. "So, where are these facilities you already showed me?" I demanded. Les just stared at me. I could see the clear lid of his large oval eyes blinking quickly as his mouth fell agape.

I turned to Tikk who responded, "Yes, of course." Tikk grabbed me by the arm and lead me out of the room. As soon as we turned the corner Tikk began to giggle and said, "I cannot believe you spoke to him like that. He is furious with you."

I stumbled after him and said, "Well, I mean... this place is confusing, and I do really have to go… and..." I was still focused on my bladder but the thought of that massive creature being angry with me was taking my mind off just how much I needed to expel waste. "Do you think…"

"Here we are." Tikk had turned me into one of the seemingly invisible doorways and we were standing in yet another white cube of a room. "I'll give you a quick lesson on using the facilities. It should sense your needs just as it does ours. Our systems are so similar I'm sure it will just assume you are a Par female."

As he spoke a cylindrical silver tube raised from the floor right behind me. I was correct in assuming this was my new toilet, and despite the lack of real seat, water, or flush, it looked like it would do the trick.

"So, you are going to disrobe and sit there to do your business. When you are complete wait for the device to cleanse you. From the facilities on your ship it is clear your species has not figured out metalight cleansing technology yet." Tikk was standing right next to me and now appeared to be waiting for me to get to it. I was a science experiment; I got it, and I would have wanted to watch him pee if our positions had been switched, but I still didn't want to give him a show. "Could you leave or turn around or something? I don't think I'll even be able to go with you watching like that."

"I'm sorry." His hands shot up in defense like I was about to smack him. "I'm sorry, I was curious about what you looked like, but, yes, that is rude. I have an issue with this; separating science and a creature's individual identity." With that he walked out of the room and turned the corner. I pushed the lack of privacy out of my mind and let my thoughts rest on Tikk's words as I relieved myself. An alien creature that I still saw as more thing than individual had just recognized the legitimacy of my existence.

Tikk also showed me the full body metalight cleanser

and how to use it. I walked into the bright orange light and allowed the beam to do its job. Even my teeth could be cleaned by the beam of light by simply opening my mouth until a disembodied voice deemed me "harmful bacteria-free." I was beginning to appreciate the Par's use of colors, and I felt cleaner than I had in many years. This was also the beginning of my hair issues, and Tikk's fascination with the filaments that sprouted all over my body. We both spent a few moments raking our fingers through the tangled mess on top of my head, but I was excited to keep moving.

Tikk had gotten me some new clothes while I was being cleaned. He did a good job of altering them, so I didn't have any excess material hanging down my back.

"The females of our species do not have fat on their chests." Tikk nodded towards my breasts as he said this. I was standing naked in front of him at this point, but I had stopped caring by then. "And the majority of them have physical modifications. Most often jewelry. So, it would be pointless for them to cover themselves with excess clothing. Also, your species skin is far weaker than our own. You must come from a very hospitable planet. What is the purpose of your alterations; are they purely for aesthetics like the jewels Par females have implanted in their skin?" Tikk reached out and stroked the phoenix tattoo on my forearm. I had not thought of its significance in many years. Tikk continued, "I am sorry. I didn't mean to pry. Your alterations are very lovely. Very full of color." He pushed the black clothing into my palms.

"I forget I have these things sometimes." I motioned to the five permenant markings that covered different parts of my body. Each represented an aspect of my life that I wasn't ready to get into at that the moment. I grabbed the clothes from him. "Thanks for this." I pulled the tiny shorts on; then lifted the thin black strip of material to eye level. I pulled the small elastic top over my head, and the spandex-like material clung to my body. It was and still is the best support my body has ever received. I looked at Tikk and gave him my most dazzling smile in hopes I would win his heart the same way he had mine. I then started to wonder if he in fact had a literal heart, or if he had some other muscle that pumped some unique kind of life sustaining chemical throughout his body.

Instead of asking one of the many biological questions flipping around in my brain I went with, "This material is amazing, what is it made of?"

"The Philex?" He stepped closer and took my arm. "Come I'll take you to a sleep chamber. There is time for you to rest."

He guided me out of the facility room and down the hallway as he answered my question. "The Philex is harvested from a plant grown on a planet named Trallcore. It was the first planet the Par Scanning Troops came across back when our space exploration program was in its first three hundred years. We were lucky to find a life sustaining planet so early, and one even more hospitable to life than our own."

We stopped abruptly. "This room will do fine." He adjusted me so he was looking directly into my eyes now, "Do not fear your future, your species will survive." Tikk turned me around to enter the room.

A small bed folded out of the wall. "Wait here, I forgot your evening meal." He turned the corner and was gone for a short amount of time and returned with a glass of thick blue liquid. "This is full of nutrients and will help you sleep. I do not know what you usually consume, but your genetic makeup is similar enough to my own that I know this will support your immune system. Please rest now. You will be sent for once we have reached your planet." He turned and I made one last ditch effort to keep him there. I feared being alone with my thoughts.

"So those spikey on your back, are they also modifications like my markings?" He turned back to me and tilted his head.

"Our spears are additions to our bodies; they are for protective purposes. Our species also makes use of vain alterations, but never for coordinates the way you do. Why would you permanently print the location of a dead planet on your foot?"

Every Searcher gets a permanent imprint of their birth planet and Earth's coordinates before heading into space in hopes that at least the body can be returned if it is found. I looked down at the strange liquid in my hand and my stomach churned. I was starving but the pungent odor of the blue goo was confusing my senses. I knew I had to drink it, but I didn't want Tikk to watch my face as I gagged on his offering.

"Thank you for being so helpful and for the drink. I am really hungry, and really tired now that I have had a moment to think about it." I sat down on the bed.

"Then I shall leave you Elinor. It is thrilling to come into contact with you." Tikk nodded his head and left.

I glared down at the turquoise concoction that smelled like a mixture of rotten meat and boiled greens. I sighed and contemplated my options. Then I quickly decided that my options were shit and not the best pre-nap-time concentration, and so I focused on the challenge at hand.

Deep breath. Chug it.

It didn't taste as bad as it smelled; it was the chunky texture that was so foreign, but my body was immediately satisfied, and as soon as my hunger was satiated, I could feel exhaustion settle in around me. I pulled back a light pink blanket, identical to the one Urral gave me earlier, and curled up on the bed. The soft foam of the mattress contoured to my body. Before I could begin to ponder the meaning of everything that had just happened, I was asleep.

5.

I awoke completely aware of my surroundings. My mind's ability to remain calm and alert was exasperating. Sometimes a girl just wants to sink into a state of shock-induced unconsciousness.

I was sitting up in my small bed when Tikk poked his head through the large opening, and said, "You are awake." He smiled a shockingly toothy grin and entered the room.

"What is it with the whole hiding everything in the walls and no closed-off rooms thing you guys have going on?" I swept the room with my arms. "How do I ever find this room again? I'd end up walking into the med bay when I need the toilet if I lived here." I looked at Tikk and wondered if we had arrived at Kepler yet, but I was more interested in learning about my hosts than getting back to my useless planet.

"The bareness of our ship upsets you. Les and I spoke of your little outburst while you were asleep." I inhaled quickly upon remembering how I had yelled at the purple beast in my bladder bursting rage.

Tikk saw my look of fear and reassured me, "It is expected for cultures to clash when first coming into contact with each other. Misunderstandings are part of the process and easily forgiven. We are a warrior species. Since birth, Kara warriors are trained for combat and taught to be ready for any situation. We evolved with little need for sitting. The Harlukkna are a peaceful, research based culture; you will be introduced to them in due time. They have architecture more conducive to sitting and privacy. Closing off rooms would not suit the sense of camaraderie our culture wishes to uphold, and it would hinder us if the ship were under attack. We respect each other's privacy and never enter another's personal space without them being aware, but there is not great need for personal space among our kind."

Tikk stretched his hand out to me. "Would you like to join us on the deck? Your planet should be coming into view soon."

I placed my pale hand in his green, callused one. The lines on his palm could have belonged to any human; if that human had three long fingers instead of four and black, unbreakable nails, but we both had thumbs that could clasp the other's hand. Par skin is similar in form to human skin but feels as if it was covered with a few centimeters of tar, thick and impenetrable.

Tikk pulled me to standing and said, "As for knowing what rooms are where, that just takes time like when you enter any new place. It is simple when you understand the lay out. We are currently in the living-quarters section of the ship, which is the upper portion. Each portal opens to either a sleeping or facility room down this hall, and your room will now recognize you. When you approach, the lights will illuminate. If you enter a facility room and do not need to use any of the devices then nothing will happen and you will know where you are."

"Well, at least I'll be able to find my room again." I

smiled at this small comfort as we exited and turned right. "So, are we walking towards the area where the control and medical rooms are?"

"Yes, can you feel the floor slant down?" I could feel a slant in the floor but it seemed too slight to make much of a difference.

"We are descending into the main area of the ship now. The ship is made of a Philect similar to the fibers our clothes are made from, but with a different chemical base. It gives the ship a malleable texture that can be manipulated and made to fit into whatever shape is most needed at any given moment. The ship's usual shape looks a bit like this," He held up his free hand and pointed two fingers while spreading them apart to make a 'V.'

He continued. "With the control room located at the center and the living and storage sections of the ship breaking off in separate directions. There are times when we need more space in the medical bay and so that space is taken from the storage area because they both run along the same section of the ship, and, if necessary, the medical bay can give up space to the hanger."

He must have seen the awe on my face because he let out a small gurgling laugh and said, "The way I am explaining it must make it sound fantastical, but I promise everything can be easily explained with simple physics, but I fear that it would not be so simple to you." He smiled at me then and I could see a glimpse of sympathy in his eyes.

"Another reason we prefer to keep a common color and design throughout the ship is so that those not familiar with the layout are easily confused. No species has ever been able to take a Par ship while Par still inhabited it. Les, we are here." I hadn't noticed that we were standing at the entrance to the control room until Tikk informed Les of our arrival.

Les was even more intimidating than I remembered. He was not the tallest of his crew. In fact he was about medium height for the Par, but Les demanded attention. His gaze rested on me and I suddenly forgot there was anyone else in the room. For a being I had considered monstrous just a few fractions ago Les was very aesthetically appealing to me at the moment. Perhaps it had something to do with my planet, bright blue Kepler, looming at me from the window behind him, or perhaps it was the way his upper nostrils began to pulse as he stared at me.

As I tore my eyes from Les' amethyst form to scan the room I realized that all their faces were more human that I had first thought. Their eyes: large, black, and upturned were gorgeously alien, but the gill-like nostrils took more time to acquire a taste for.

Les had a wide jaw, which only added to his animalistic appearance. Urral, and the majority of the crew, had longer more human features, but all of their noses were flat against their face, and equipped with a second pair of slits. I found myself staring at them constantly.

The extra slits on Les' nose were going bat shit when

my eyes returned to his face, and I was reminded of Tikk's existence when he spoke into my left ear. "We are ready to land, but Les and I would like to discuss our plans with you before we arrive. We have learned through experience that colonization is eased with communication. We have identified 71 life forms that match your genetic code residing on the planet, but the planet itself is not altogether hospitable." Les had begun to approach us as Tikk spoke.

Les stopped just short of my right shoulder. I could have reached out and stroked his thick skin. "Have you informed her of our plans?" He asked Tikk. Now that he was standing two inches from me I had become invisible.

"I was just starting to. I thought it would be best if we both spoke to her." Tikk was still linked to my left arm and he began to pet my hand as if I needed consoling. Now they both turned to face me and Tikk said, "Elinor, you and your people do not wish to remain on your planet, correct?" This was the negotiation.

"No, of course not." With those four words I had already lost. These guys weren't here to save us. They were here to profit off of us. I continued with caution, "This planet, Kepler, was only meant to be a settler colony while the process of terraformation was carried out. Earth, our planet of origin, had begun the process of colonizing other planets for natural materials with the hope of one day housing humans for the long term, but the colonies were never meant to be replacements for Earth."

Les' face tilted in confusion and I pushed forward

with the gory details. "My species had outgrown and over developed our planet. We needed a place to put all the excess people and also an answer to the food shortage problem. About two hundred years ago our scientists discovered a way to harness the sun's energy in a way that powered our spacecraft beyond anything we had known before."

I met Tikk's shocked gaze. He shook his head in confusion and said, "You used the star that warmed your own planet for energy? Even a massive and young star would be drained in a matter of…"

I nodded in agreement. "And that's exactly what happened. We had only set up three colonies by the time the sun started to wane. The effects on Earth were of course catastrophic and everyone that could afford it escaped to one of the fledgling colonies, but obviously none of them were ready to maintain life. From what we could glean from the small amount of communication we received from the other two we are the only survivors. It wasn't like we didn't have any warning. My father remembered physicists predicting the inevitable and numerous attempts to stop technology from progressing, but who wants to listen to hippies and scientists when there are millions of dollars to be made. The people of Earth knowingly fucked themselves over." I stopped abruptly. Tikk and Les both shifted uneasily at my use of profanity. I again became aware that I was speaking in their language with such ease, and the word for fuck in their language is melodic when compared to its harsh parallel in my first language, English.

"Your species destroyed its own planet." I saw awe in Les' face as he spoke. I could feel the tensions around us shift as they reconsidered me. Humans had become something dangerous to them. "We assumed we had found fellow colonizers, but this is…" Les fell silent but kept his eyes on me as he thought. Tikk began to tighten his grip on my arm as if preparing to move me quickly.

Then Les broke our staring competition by yelling, "Prepare the cargo ships for departure." Tikk pulled me out of the room.

Les followed us and Tikk took over the conversation. "We are going to take three cargo ships down to load your people. We will not be staying on the planet for more than two fractions."

We entered the cargo hold and I saw my pod sitting in the corner. It looked jagged and tiny next to the massively cylindrical cargo ships Tikk was pointing toward. The cargo hold itself was cavernous and held more than just the four ships. The first half of the room was obviously for storage and was what appeared to be the only closed off room on the ship.

"You will of course come with us. We will need you to translate until we can get your humans on board and injected with LiquiParian. We now know that it takes about ten fractions for your body to assimilate the serum. Please, step up here." Tikk lead me to the side of one of the huge, oblong white ships and was motioning for me to enter a curved opening that revealed a porcelain white interior.

I nodded as I placed my hand on the outer wall of the ship. “Who does your cleaning?” I asked, laughing at the silliness of my question because no one else did.

I stepped into the circular vessel. I felt like I was inside a slightly flattened sphere. Again, the area was bare and a large viewing portal showed me a view of the cargo bay. I walked further in as Tikk, Les, and Urral entered the ship behind me. "How do you keep everything so white?" I touched one of the malleable walls; the surface was gritty, not smooth, as I had assumed.

"It is the same material the main ship is made from. It absorbs any residue that remains on it for longer than a couple fractions." Urral answered me. He smiled and turned toward the portal where Tikk was programming the Zorb. A small control panel slide out from the wall beside the viewing portal and the Zorb broke into millions of tiny pieces within the blue ray of light projecting from the panel.

The ship was beginning to buzz and click and I could feel a jolt as the Zorb broke up. "Please, everyone take a position," Tikk said as he led me by my shoulder towards the back wall.

He turned me to face him and then pushed my back so that I touched the wall. Upon making contact the wall became soft and dough like. I felt like I was being pushed into a sponge, and when I was one with the wall, Tikk released me. I was about halfway into the wall and could feel it gripping me, but I also felt that I could easily pull away if I desired.

"These ships go beyond fast. The bending of space can be unpredictable and can bend the body as well if precauciones are not taken. It is best that we do not have any option for individual movement while we are in Zorb leap." Tikk smiled at me and then leaned himself against the part of the wall to my right. I could see Les and Urral doing the same thing on the other side.

"So, can the entire ship do this? Like in my room or the med bay?" The ship began to humm once everyone was secure. It was the last time I would ever land on Kepler.

"You mean secure our bodies?" Tikk answered. I could hear Urral and Les discussing something about food rations and my stomach growled. "Yes, your bed secured you during our leap here. You were just unaware of it."

"This is far superior to anything my people ever designed."

It felt as it I blinked, and the ship was suddenly hovering about three hundred kilometers above what was left of my human settlement on Kepler, and I had not sensed any shift in speed.

"We use the same material in all our ships, and in most of our homes on Qualittia. The wall becomes malleable as the ship prepares for takeoff. It is not used for that purpose on Qualittia, our planet," He added to answer my questioning gaze. "You can step out now. The ship will lower to the ground slowly."

Les and Urral had already stepped away from the

wall and were walking toward the front of the ship. I pushed myself out with ease and joined them to gaze at pathetic looking settlement.

"Your colony is within range and should be aware of our arrival. Do you believe they will attempt to attack us as we descend?" Les turned to face me as he spoke. Tikk had moved to my left, so Les and I stood close to each other with the other two males flanking us.

"I don't believe they would even be able to." I replied. "We used to have many powerful weapons and ammunition, but all legitimate fire power was used up during the last rebellion."

"You used weapons on your own kind? It is no wonder your population has gotten so dangerously low," Urral snorted in a laugh at the absurdity of my statement. He was right; we were not an intelligent species.

"When we land, you must do as I say and act quickly." Les said. I nodded and watched my people make their way towards the ship. A fear came over me stronger than anything I had felt with the Par. The thought of communicating with my own species was more difficult than meeting a new one.

JUDAS

6.

The oblong Par ship landed outside of the settlement known as CenCast3 and I could see a crowd forming. A disembodied voice began to inform us that the atmosphere was not sufficient. Tikk walked back to the wall that had secured us during flight, which slid open to reveal storage. I mimicked Tikk by picking up one of the clear masks that hung now on the wall. As I examined the translucent mask, I considered what I would say to my brother. I had been a long time away from home.

"The mask should fit you. Hold it in front of your face and it will shift to fit your small features. It will allow you to breath on planet."

Tikk was putting his mask on as he said this. Les and Urral already wore theirs and were watching me. I lifted the transparent mask to my face and could see it come to life. It flexed and reached for me while it shrank to fit snuggly around the edges of my hair line and jaw. As soon as my mask was on, the door opened and we all stepped out into the light.

I brought my hand up to shield my eyes as they adjusted to Kepler's sun, which is slightly closer than Earth's and Qualittia 's. The colony had to move the settlement twice a year in order to stay on the area of the planet not tilted directly toward the star. On paper Kepler was a perfect planet for terraformation. The climate was mild and livable, but in reality the soil was useless and needed thousands of years in order to be ready for sustaining oxygen based life. We were never able to grow anything and had wasted millions of gallons of water, shipped from Earth, in the process of trying. The small aquifers native to the planet had dried up within a couple years, and the suns proximity made rain nearly impossible.

I looked out on a dwindling settlement made up of three cylindrical-shaped tent structures. There had been over one hundred tents in the original colony. What appeared to be the entire population of CenCast were huddled together in their bulky walking suits about ten meters from the three ships. No one spoke and I pushed my way past the Par in order to make myself visible.

My brother was the first to recognize me. "Elinor!" Judas ran towards me and threw his long arms around my shoulders before I had a chance to respond. His walking suit made it an awkward hello but I didn't mind the cumbersome embrace.

"Elinor, what are you doing here? What the fuck are you wearing?" His light blue eyes whipped about as he tried to take in the Par and me at the same time. "Who are these guys? Are you ok?"

Judas had stepped back but still had a grip on my shoulders.

"I'm fine, and these guys are here to save us," I said, awkwardly tugging on my shorts as I motioned to the colorful giants standing behind me. "They're called the Par. They're from a planet called Qualittia, and I really don't think they want to hurt us, but… I did it…I found something."

Everyone else was starting to crowd in now. Les and the other Par backed up towards the rear of their ship. The eyes of every human followed them.

"So… so, this is it." Judas' eyes widened and his arms followed suit. I could feel another hug on the horizon. "You did it El. You fucking found something....someone." And there was the hug. He looked at the gathering crowd. "Hey, back up. It's El! She found these guys! She brought them here to save us!" He was screaming and waving his hands above his head at this point. I could see familiar faces but had I been off planet for eight years.

Everyone had gotten so old.

I saw my one friend, Ming, in the crowd and reached out for her. I hadn't grown close to most of my fellow CenCast residents. I had been raised very separate from them, and when everything came crashing down I signed up for the Searchers and spent most of my life off planet. My brother had earned the love of these people but I never even tried.

"Look at you, beautiful girl." Ming pulled me into her small, soft body. "You have returned to us and brought our salvation with you." When she pulled away there were tears in her almond eyes. Ming touched my face and began to laugh. "Are they going to say anything to us, or just scare everyone with their big, black eyes?" Her hand swept towards the colorful monstrosities lingering in the background.

I turned to see Tikk, Urral, and Les inching closer to the murmuring crowd. I broke from Ming's grasp and made my way toward them.

"Wait a second." I put my hand on Tikk's chest and heard a reaction from the crowd of on lookers as they heard me speak Parian.

I told Tikk, "I still don't really know the general consensus yet."

Then I turned back to the group of nervous humans and shouted, "As you can see I have come back from my Search with a solution, our only solution. The Par have offered to take us with them, back to their planet, which they have assured me will sustain us. They do not want to stay here longer than a few hours. I know this is sudden, but you need to prepare yourselves to leave now." I looked back at Tikk to find Les behind me.

"What have you said to them?" He again placed himself very close to me, and my right shoulder was currently brushing against the center of his chest. I made no attempt to move away but instead leaned my head back in order to meet his eyes.

"I told them to pack and be ready to leave soon. I said you were going to take us back to your planet which is life sustaining." I was looking up at him and felt his hand rest on my lower back.

"How do we know these things don't just want to eat us or something? I know Kepler can't sustain us but what if we go with these guys and end up dinner?"

I didn't know the woman that vocalized the human's fears, but she made her point and murmurs rose up around her. A middle aged man with a hooked nose added, "Look at her. They've probably brain washed her by now."

I stepped away from Les and moved in the direction of the thin man. Judas spit out the man's name as he stepped between the crowd and me, "Luke, how dare you make assumptions about my sister after she has brought us an answer; a solution to our problem. It's go with these guys or stay here and die. Yes, it's a risk leaving the planet and neither El nor I can make any promises but staying on Kepler is death. This is our only chance and you all know that. I bet they know it too." He jerked his thumb over his shoulder in the Par's direction. "Do you really want to start this interaction with a fight?"

"I'm with Judas," Another older woman spoke up. "I want my children to have a chance to live, and to have the possibility to have children of their own. Come on boys." She said the last part to the three men standing beside her. There were no more children in CenCast. Judas was the youngest person on planet and yet he appeared to hold quite a bit of power over these seemingly broken people. Other groups concurred and broke off towards the living chamber.

Judas nudged my shoulder with his. "Come on sis. Let's go grab my stuff. What's the weird thing between you and the purple guy?" I attempted to interject but Judas ignored my look of indignation and pulled me into him as we walked. "Then you can give me a tour of one of those crazy ass spaceships."

I turned and looked behind us at Les who was standing akimbo looking very disheartened. I answered his disgruntled stare by saying, "We'll be back quickly. Everyone is going to get their belongings. Just wait a bit.

I wrapped my arm around Judas' waist and allowed him to lead me away before Les could open his mouth. Judas led me toward the tent on our right while everyone else headed toward the tent on our left. "Got your own place or something?" I nudged him in the rib.

"Kind of; I set up a cot in the medical bay to be close to the radio in case you needed to communicate."

He opened the hatch and we entered the air tight

chamber.

"Guess that feeling in my gut was legitimate after all." He patted some of the equipment and asked, "So you only found those guys yesterday? How did you get back here so quickly? Was their planet one of the ones on the scan?"

He spoke as he started to throw random items into a blue satchel. I thought to tell him all of these things were pointless now but I didn't want to thrust him into the reality of the situation just yet. Judas was excited and when we got excited we started to talk very fast, but even when no one else could, my brother and I always understood each other.

"Actually, they found my ship about twelve hours ago. Obviously, they have crazy technology that I can in no way understand or explain, and part of that technology involves bending space. I'm sure Tikk will be happy to give you a run down when we get back to the main ship."

Judas cocked his head at me from the other side of the room.

I said, "Tikk is the green guy. The purple one is Les and the pink is Urral. There are only twelve male crew members on board this massive ship. I don't remember all their names."

"You've never been good with names. I bet you don't know anyone but me and Ming out there." Judas zipped up his bag and I followed him out.

"I've spent maybe a total of eighteen of the last forty-eight years on planet, and most of that was spent locked away in the old house."

He sent me a disapproving look as he opened the outside hatch. "No excuses; just own it. I love you but you can be a bit of a cunt at times." I punched his shoulder as he swung the door shut. "Guess there's no point in locking up or anything now. Probably never see this rock again, huh?" He swung the small bag around in a circle and let it go. "I'll never need any of that stuff again either will I?" He motioned toward the bag as it landed behind him in the dust.

"No, I don't think our tablets would work on Qualittia. I think everything is about to change." I nudged him in the ribs again because it made me feel like things weren't as serious as they were. "Oh crap, I forgot I was the only one that could communicate with them." I spotted a small group of people creeping closer to the waiting ships, with fear plastered across their faces, and rushed over to help Tikk corral them into the back entrances.

"Let me help. Where do you need them to go?" I asked Tikk as I approached the scared looking crowd.

"Thank you." Tikk looked equally nervous surrounded by all the humans in their suits. "I was concerned they would reach us before you did, and I did not know how to tell them I needed them to leave all their belongings here. Clothing, food, shelter will all be provided for them once they are settled on Qualittia-- or Trallcore, and their waste will be used to charge a Zorb."

Tikk swung his head around and walked toward the back of the ship. The humans had arms full of the same things Judas had originally thought to bring. All the useless crap we put meaning into because it was ours. I locked eyes with the woman closest to me and said, "You can't bring any of that with you. I'm sorry. I know I said to get your things, but the Par said that you will not need any of it anyway." More people with random, useless stuff cradled lovingly in their arms were arriving. Judas was telling everyone to drop their bags.

"Come on guys. There's really no point right? The tablets have been useless for years now. We're going to have new identities when we get there. Be new people." Judas always said things in the right way.

Ming tossed her bag to the ground and walked up to meet me. "What do I need any of that for anyway? I want some of those tiny shorts you're wearing." She stuck her index finger into the top of my shorts, pulled it towards her, and let it go pop back onto my hipbone. She raised her eyebrows and whispered, "Sexy." I couldn't help laughing, but as I pushed her away because I was thoroughly embarrassed.

"This is all they have."

"If you think I'm crawling into those teeny tiny things you are bat shit crazy," Judas said coming between us, satisfied that everyone was calmly discarding their now worthless belongings.

"Don't focus on the clothes right now, ok? Think about stuff like oxygen and the ability to cultivate crops and help me organize everyone along the walls of the back of the ship." Judas broke into action immediately, and I saw Les exit the front of the ship and catch sight of me. "We're loading up."

Les walked toward me as I spoke.

"How did you learn their language so quickly?" Ming remained by my side and was watching our exchange in awe.

"They injected me with this stuff. Not pretty but it works. I think you are all going to get injected at some point." I shifted my attention back to Les.

He stopped further from me than I had expected. "We are ready. Have the… what do you call yourselves?" Les looked at Ming then back at me. "You are young compared to the rest of your species."

"I didn't age normally while I was out on Search. This is Ming." I waved my hand between his torso and hers. "Ming, this is Les." I was able to jump between our languages with ease now. "He's kind of in charge around here."

I wrinkled my nose and rolled my eyes as much to put her at ease as to annoy him. Then I turned back to Les and said, "We call ourselves humans. I'll have everyone line up outside the cargo chambers."

Les called after us as we made our way to the back of the ships. "Inform them of how to secure themselves into the walls. Also have them remove their bulky suites and throw them out for the Zorb. You will be riding back with us in the main chamber."

I screamed from about ten meters away, "I'll stay with them. In case they get scared or want to ask any questions." I slowly walked backwards as Ming joined Judas in his attempts to keep everyone calm and coordinated.

Les took a couple steps forward and said, "No" in a low, vehement tone I had not heard before. It suited him. He closed the gap between us and continued. "I will help you organize the… humans," The word was difficult for him to say. "Then we will return to the main chamber." He walked past me before I could say another word.

7.

The leap back to the main ship was a continuation of the previous scene and Les' strange behavior. Tikk had wordlessly moved so that Les and I were pressed into the wall close together, and when I asked when we expected to arrive on their planet it was Les that spoke up.

"We need to collect sufficient power before we are ready for the Zorb leap. We will send a Zorb to absorb all the waste your species has somehow been unable to dispose of properly. It should be about ten fractions before we are prepared to leap. Do not worry. Your people will be secured." Les saying all of this only made me feel more concerned. It was very possible nothing would work out the way I was hoping.

"And once we are on planet?" I asked as we popped into the cargo bay of the main ship. My question went unanswered.

The main ship was a huge acute angle but the connecting point was rounded and black while the lines forming the angle were the same bright white as everything else. It certainly stuck out in its surroundings. The black was obviously due to the massive portal in the control center, and I could make out a dotted line of black rectangles that were the various viewing portals in all the rooms lining the hallways. I pulled myself from the wall and jumped out of the hatch as soon as it opened. I wanted to be the first one out so I could organize the unloading. There was plenty of room in the cargo area for everyone to stand comfortably, but I didn't know where we would put them for the eventual Zorb leap. Les and Tikk were following close behind me and so I turned to ask, "Where should I tell them to go? Do they need to be injected with your language first?"

We had rounded the ship and Les lifted his hand above his head and swiped in a downward motion. The back of the ship began lowering to reveal the people pressed against the walls inside.

"Just push yourselves away from the wall. You should come away easily." They did as I said and started to move forward gingerly. "Wait." I waved my hands so those in the back could see and turned to Les. "Well, where do I take them?"

"To the holding chambers at the back wall." Les motioned with his arm and then began to walk towards the cargo area where two large, clear barriers flanked a wall. "They will be secure and out of the way here." He did the same up-down hand motion as before and wall that separated the two transparent barriers slid into the floor. He stepped into the large, enclosed room and spread his arms in approval.

"There are facilities and food supplies if they need them." Judas was making his way around reiterating my instructions. I found Ming and enlisted her help in having everyone make their way towards the enclosed room along the back wall.

"They want everyone to go into that holding chamber." I held her arm and pointed toward where Les stood. "There is food and toilets, and beds, so everyone will be safe during the leap in there."

She glared in Les' direction. "Looks kind of like a jail cell or a science exhibit." Her face turned back to me. "Do you trust these guys not to kill us, or ... I don't know... do something really bad."

Even though we were separated from the group I lowered my voice. "I have no idea what is going to happen, but I do know we have no real option here. Let's just get everyone settled and I can start trying to get more information out of them." I attempted a smile then turned to the crowd of frightened looking people in the middle of the cargo bay.

"Ok everyone, you see that opening. That's our luxury accommodations; we will be safe in there during the leap. It won't take long." I could feel my frustration at their blank stares growing, but thankfully Judas stepped in.

"Ok," Judas exclaimed as he stood up. "Li family, the Zhaos, Jacobsons, the Jiangs, Duskys, Monroes, and the Lynn family, stop staring at me and move your butts into the room. I need to use one of those toilets." Ming grabbed her cousin by the elbow and began walking towards the chamber and the crowd shuffled into motion. Judas stopped next to me as everyone else made their way towards what could very easily be the last room they ever stayed in. "You and I are the only Sturgeons left." He cocked his head to the right and gave my shoulder another light punch. "I'm assuming you're going to go talk to our saviors?" Judas motioned behind me and as I turned I could see Les standing near the exit to the hallway glaring in our direction.

"Yeah, I'll come find you when I've gotten a bit more information about what they intend on doing with us." I hesitated, wanting to spend more time with him. "Hopefully you will all get injected with their language at some point so I don't have to keep acting as the go between."

I turned back to find Les' stance unchanged and cut the interaction short.

"It's really nice to see you, Judas." I returned his shoulder punch and joined Les at the opening to the hallway.

Once all the humans had made their way inside, two Par crew members, one dark red named Runn and the other bright orange named Innc, swiped hands along the wall and the wall reappeared. Innc and Runn stood outside the chambers while the rest of the crew made their way out of the cargo area. Les waited for me beside the exit.

"I don't see why you have to lock them in and set up a guard." I stopped short, placed my hands on my hips, and made what I hoped was a disapproving look. "It's not like they have anywhere to go."

"Come, it has been a long day and we must eat." He turned and began walking down the hallway before I could respond, so I followed him but made certain to stomp as loudly as possible in protest. Les lead me in the direction of the main deck but passed it and turned into the first room down the living corridor. It was yet another large white room, but there was a long table in the middle of this one. Still no chairs but the shelves on the left sidewall were filled with what had to be food and cooking utensils. The Par's food is as colorful as they are. Bright blue, green, and orange melons sat in a bowl. Slices of protien that was more purple than red were laid out on a white counter top. The grey colored Cykk was busy cutting up yellow bushels of leaves as Tikk looked on.

Les approached Tikk and asked, "Will there be sufficient fuel?" Tikk was standing near a small grey hole in the wall that I assumed lead to a Zorb and was using a silver tool to crush the yellow florets into liquid.

Tikk put down the juicing machine and turned to face us. "Yes, and then some; we will be in Sharronn within eight fractions." Tikk seemed to notice me for the first time and jumped into action. "I'm sure you are very hungry. Rehydrate first." He handed me a jar which I placed under the small faucet that was located beside the waste receptacle.

"Did you enjoy the mixture I gave you before?" Tikk grabbed the device that rested on the counter beside him. He held it out so I could see a small amount of yellow liquid sloshing around in a jar connected to the bottom of the apparatus. "Very delicious and efficient form of consumption."

My stomach grumbled and I was reminded of that fact that I hadn't really eaten all day. "Uh, is this the only stuff you guys have? What will the rest of the humans be given?" There were five other crew members in the room leaning against the table and drinking multi-colored pulpy mixtures from large jugs.

"This is the best way to transport and consume food while on long leap missions. Liquid is easily derived from our own waste water and moisture collected from the juice plants, but most of our storage space is used for our supply chamber, which is filled with our frozen produce and protein. When the food is crystalized it is easier to store and to break down into its basic nutrient rich form when prepared for consumption, but that means it must be prepared while still frozen and so becomes juice extract. We are able to consume less and gain more."

Tikk returned to his compressing and looked over my head at Les. "Do you want to join us in the recreation room after this? I do not plan on training long, but the exercise will help me sleep."

He removed the now full jar from the device and poured half of its contents into a separate container and handed it to me. "You are also welcome to come, or you may return to the humans. I promise Innc and Runn are taking good care of them, and Cykk is preparing enough sustenance for all to be satisfied. We gain nothing if they are not healthy and impressive specimens."

He chugged his drink down and handed me a sample, which I raised to my lips for a small sip. My face contorted into a crumpled grimace before I could help myself. "Oh man, I guess the best way to go with this stuff is to avoid all olfactory interaction whatsoever." I held the liquid as far from my body as I could. Les and

Tikk tilted their heads in confusion.

"It is consumed for its nutritional value not its odor." Les was in the process of making his own concoction as he said this.

"Do you not like the taste? Juwakkwon beast is my favorite of the quadrupeds." Tikk shrugged his shoulders and finished the last of his in one slurping gulp.

"I don't mean to be picky. It's very filling, thank you." I held my breath as I tilted the contents of my cup toward my mouth and followed it immediately with a gulp of water. "And I would like to join you in the recreation room if you don't mind. If you're willing to teach me how to use whatever weird machines you have down there."

I tipped the remainder of the yellow pulp down my throat and tried to drink it all before it registered on my taste buds. There was a recreation area in my pod and I had always been active despite my years in stasis. I could tell by the physical condition of my new companions, that the Par value a fit body even more than humans do.

"You are more than welcome, and our form of exercise is simple to learn. Les?"

Tikk took the now empty container from my hand and tossed both towards the hole on the back of the cabinet. Les' liquid meal was purple and nearly the same shade as himself. This juxtaposition lead to my questioning the origins of the Par's magnificent fluctuation in color tone, which inevitably lead to me smiling in wonder at my new life.

Les threw his empty container in the same disposal hole and said, "What pleases you?"

Both he and Tikk angled themselves toward me. I was taken aback by being caught, but they both grinned as if waiting for me to tell them a joke.

"I was..." I reminded myself that the only dumb question is the one not asked and so I continued, "What gives you your pigment? Is it the food you eat?" I indicated the colorful, frozen bounty laid out on the counter.

Both males burst into laughter and I was left without an answer while they scoffed. Tikk was the first to notice my disgruntled stance.

He calmed down and answered, "Our pigmentation is by choice. Mostly parents choose it when their child is born, but it is fairly easy to have your pigmentation changed if you wish."

"How do you do it?"

"An injection into the spine, similar to the one used to inject you with LiquiParin. The brain then directs the injection to the epidermis where it is assimilated."

"You got a pigment change, right?" Les asked Tikk.

"Yes, my parents chose blue, but I just never felt that was really my color." Tikk and Les shared a look that indicated that they knew something and were not inclined to let me in on it.

"What do you look like without the color?"

"Par's epidermis is naturally black or grey, like Cykk." As Tikk answered he looked to Cykk who nodded at me in return.

“I have no intentions of ever altering my tone.” Cykk reminded us of the pride he took in his natural form.

Les spoke up. "It seems as if all our recent inventions have been directed at physical beauty" He shifted his feet and rolled his large shoulders. "We have given up on progressing our cause or regaining our dignity. Now all the Par want are jewel implants and the brightest epidermis." His eyes caught my own and for a moment I think I saw shame. "Even a civilization as advanced as ours is obsessed with the superficial."

"Fine, Les, we all know of your distaste for the Par's obsession with physical appearance, but not all of us are genetically disposed to be beautiful the way you were, and your parents chose such a magnificent color for you." Tikk beamed at his commander and patted him on the arm as if comforting an elderly female. My mouth could not help but fall open as I marveled at the way Tikk teased the male I supposed a tyrant.

Les was satisfied with the conversation and walked toward the exit. "We will see if you can handle yourself with Par weights." This comment was obviously meant for me, and his lips formed a sly smile before he turned and left the room. Tikk nudged me with his elbow and let out one of his gurgling laughs before jogging after Les.

I followed them down the hall. When I entered the

room the expansive viewing portal that made up the wall opposite the entrance caught me off guard, but I was becoming accustomed to the feeling of entering space every time I went into a room located along the outside of the ship.

By the time Tikk and I entered Les had already began to toss around two small green spheres. Shurr and Bryyl could be seen on the far side of the large room. They had connected themselves with an expandable rope and were running in opposite directions, each trying to pull the other behind him. As I got closer to the wall on my left I could see a row of drawers full of different colored spheres.

"Fun, exercise balls. Do I just pick my favorite color?" I reached for a green ball in the far-right drawer.

"Those will be the heaviest. The yellow are the lightest and they go up as you work your way down the wall." Tikk pulled out a purple ball from the middle drawer.

As he started to handle it I could tell the spheres were malleable like most of the objects I had come into contact with since I met the Par. Tikk pushed his right hand into the ball and gripped the side. A handle formed and he lifted the weight above his head and began bending and straightening his elbow. "It just depends on what you want to do. Les and I will sometimes play a game for agility, or we work on balance and strength individually. There are also cardio tracks along the opposite wall." Tikk indicated the area where Bryyl and Shurr were pulling each other around.

"It can go in both directions simultaneously?" I waved my hands around as I continued to watch the two males running at full speed in opposite directions but neither moving from their area more than two steps.

Les laughed as he squatted with a green ball extended straight in front of his body. "That entire area is a running track. Simply begin to run and the track will register your request no matter the direction."

"Again, with the condescending voice; not necessary." As I spoke, I moved to the right side of the room. I thought of running and felt the floor shift backwards. I picked up my feet and began to walk then jog as the floor moved away from me quicker.

"An intuitive treadmill." I exclaimed as I noticed the floor only quickened to a pace that pushed me but did not cause me to overexert myself as it shifted to create an incline.

"It is a running track." Les corrected as he sat the green ball down and moved toward the water faucet indention.

"I know." I said, without taking my eyes off the stars outside the window. "Humans had something like these and it was called a treadmill. I don't really understand the name now that I think of it."

I kept my pace and we all remained silent for awhile. Les and Tikk shifting weights and changing positions, Shurr and Bryyl completed their competition and moved to the weight area. At one point Les pulled three green balls out of the drawer and to my amazement he started juggling them while balancing on one leg or the other. Then Tikk pushed the handles in to reform his ball and grabbed two more. He joined in with the juggling action and they began to pass the balls to each other in between juggles; I couldn't take my eyes off them. My mind began to wonder as I watched the two aliens preform their strong man act, and I then I remembered why I had joined them to begin with.

I asked both, "What do you intend to do with my people when we land on your planet?" I continued to breathe in my nose and out my mouth as calmly as possible. We were just a few buddies working out and talking about the fate of humanity. "I assume you boys do this for profit and not for the warm fuzzy feeling you get from helping others."

Neither of them stopped or even broke their gaze. Which was a good idea since there was a dangerous amount of weight flying between them.

"At this moment I don't really know." Les didn't even sound like he was out of breath. "Most likely you will be put to auction. Unless you have some hidden attributes I don't see; I believe humans will be useful for no more than manual labor of some kind, even after the language implant. I can tell from your technology that your species has nothing of real value to contribute to ours."

He let his head tilt in my direction for a moment. "If humans had all been as attractive as you I would have suggested a more leisurely line of service work, but the majority of them will most likely become general laborers on Qualittia or Trallcore." Tikk was obviously feeling the strain of the work out, but Les made no sign of tiring and it was apparent that he was in control of the game.

"You're going to sell us off like cattle? You expect us to just live out our lives as slaves?"

My outrage must have registered with the track because at first I sped up, but then the floor crawled to a halt and I stood akimbo facing the two males.

"This is bullshit. We're living creatures that deserve some kind of opportunity to prove ourselves. Educate us. At least see if we can contribute more than labor." I was waving my arms all over the place. Les grunted and both of them caught their weights. I continued my rant no longer pretending to maintain a calm demeanor.

"I get that you need to profit from this, but you can't just sell us off like that. The whole reason they all agreed to come was so that humanity could survive. If you split them up how is that going to happen?"

"It is very likely your species can breed with our own." Tikk tossed his weights back into the drawer and filled himself a jar of water. "That is probably what will happen. Our species and the Harlukkna have created a new hybrid species but can only do so through artificial means. Our anatomies are far more compatible, and your species has too few numbers to reproduce successfully. It will be interesting to see what comes of our mating."

Tikk paused with the jar raised to his lips and looked between Les and me. "I do not mean to infer that you and I will mate. That is certainly not the case. I only mean as a scientist I am interested in what a hybrid of our two species would be like." Les had set aside one weight, had given the other two handles, and was raising them above his head in a flying motion as he watched our now awkward conversation.

"So, we're going to be slaves that also get used for breeding experimentation every once in a while." My gaze shot between the two of them, and I was more aggravated by their laid back attitude than by the reality of what my people were facing.

Les finally replaced his weights and walked toward us. "I do not know why you insist on becoming upset. Your people will be sold. Most likely as laborers, some possibly as personal servants, but they will all be fed, clothed, and sheltered. They will also be given payment after they have worked off their initial purchase fee. It's all very common." Les was standing close now, and he pressed his body to mine. I could smell his sweat as he said, "You do not need to worry about any of these technicalities anyway. You have already been paid for." With that Les nodded at Tikk and made his way out of the chamber.

8.

"What the fuck do you mean he bought me?" I howled at Tikk as we stood in the living corridor. "I mean, I understand the whole process but why? What does he need me for?"

"I believe you know exactly why Les has purchased you and I do not understand why you feel the need to have me explain the situation." This was the first time Tikk had sounded anything but pleased with me. "You are an attractive female despite our species obvious differences, and Les is well within his rights." He stopped short and I bumped into him. He grabbed my shoulders and said, "It is difficult to find companionship when one is drawn to a life of space flight. It is common for a Kara warrior to purchase a companion because that is the only way to sway a female into this kind of life style. I envy Les in his luck. He has found a female that seems to enjoy a life in space, and I believe you will see you are lucky in finding him as well." He smiled and all I could fixate on were his oversized canines. He pushed me into a facility. "You should use the facilities before you join Les in his chamber."

"Do you purchase women of your own species, or just aliens?" I asked.

"There are many uneducated Par on our home planet that have more offspring than income. Their children have the option of sacrificing themselves into slavery in order to supply the rest of the family." He smiled as if he was telling me something sweet.

"That's despicable!" I recoiled in shock and continued, "How could you make them sell their own children in order to feed the rest?"

I was met with a confused cocking of Tikk's head. "It is a voluntary action. They sacrifice themselves in order to feed their family. The Par that purchases a sacrificial slave is doing the slave a great justice." He spoke with such admiration that I could not respond for a couple of moments.

"Will we all be slaves?" I finally whispered.

"You will work for clothes, lodging, food, and a small wage. It is more than many on our planet could hope for." He smiled and patted my shoulder.

Again, I was silent for a moment while my mind raced. "Well, I mean… why didn't you buy me?"

Tikk was already pulling off my clothes as the orange light of the sanitizer started to glow on my naked body. I grabbed Tikks hands as they attempted to push me toward the fiery haze. "We get along, or at least we converse. He's all grunts and glares, and most importantly… I don't want to do this. You can't…" I was bargaining for what had at one time been my basic human right, but I didn't have rights anymore. I was the alien and even worse… an alien female. I was thankful for what the Par had done for us, but I felt that my body was not proper payment for my life.

"Elinor, you have no power in this relationship." Tikk

pushed me toward the light and backed away so the machine could do its thing. "You must not think of this as negative." He smiled shyly and looked at the ground. "I am flattered by your offer but I am not interested in females sexually. I prefer the intimate company of other males." My head jerked back for a second as my mind wrapped around the idea of a gay Par, and Tikk raised his head to meet my eyes again. "Do you not find Les an attractive specimen?"

I hadn't really been thinking about sexuality when I offered up the idea of Tikk buying me. I was just looking for some control in the situation. All hopes of equality between our species was slipping from my grasp. The light that surrounded me died off, but I was unable to move. Where could I run? Tikk had no power here. My only option was to speak to Les directly.

I stepped forward and reached for my clothes. "Where is his chamber?" Tikk pulled the clothes out of reach. "You have no need for these. Follow me."

He turned, and I did as I was told while absent-mindedly running my hands through my hair. There was no accommodations made for the long fibers growing from my skull. When we reached Les' room Tikk said, "Go inside. I'm sure he'll be in shortly."

Tikk looked suddenly very uncomfortable as he clutched my clothes. "Don't make things difficult for yourself, Elinor. I know this is all happening very quickly, and that we are from such different cultures. This is obviously very strange to you and I apologize for your discomfort, but you are a part of our society now and you must obey our customs." He stroked my right arm and guided me into the room.

I took a step backwards and continued to face Tikk. "You have stolen my power, and I do not know how to get it back." My world was crumbling down around me; I had become a commodity, and the only thing I could think of was how much I would miss my alone time.

"I am glad you understand your situation. I will see you when we land on Qualittia." I entered the room and took in the space. It was at least twice the size of the sleeping chamber where I spent the previous night. As usual the wall opposite the entrance was a massive portal and the rest of the walls were white. As I entered, a bed, also much larger than the one from the night before, but with the same pink blanket, rose from the floor.

I sat on the edge of the bed and looked out the window. We were still orbiting Kepler and the ship was coming up on one of the planet's moons. I reclined on the bed in order to better enjoy the opulence that confronted me. As I turned my head I saw Les standing at the entrance with his hands behind his back. His gaze roamed across my body and I was prompted into modesty as I grabbed for the blanket.

"I apologize for startling you." He said as he backed up a bit and lowered his head. I could see him attempting to make himself smaller. "I assume Tikk explained our situation. I hope you are pleased that you will not be subjected to the process of an auction."

He took a step forward and brought his hand up to

rub the back of his head. "Are you prepared to retire for the evening?" He closed the gap between us, grabbed my elbow, and lifted me off the bed to face him. My face was only a few breaths from his lips. I placed my hands on his chest and pushed back which caused me to bump into the bed. I held my hands to my sides and pushed the air from my lungs.

"I just want to make it blatantly clear that I have zero interest in having sex with you. We don't know each other, and I believe that getting to know each other would only cause me to dislike you more."

I searched his eyes for some sign of empathy but found only confusion. His arms encompassed my body and his right hand cupped the back of my head. I kept my hands pinned to my sides as I was forced to stare into his black eyes that held nothing but the reflection of my own.

"No." I bit my lip and lost our staring contest as my eyes shifted towards the vastness of space outside the room. Les pushed his double slotted nostrils into my neck and breathed deep. His hand tangled in my hair and the room was silent as Kepler's moon passed us by. His entire body pulsed around my own and our chests pushed against each other as we battled for oxygen.

He spoke softly into my ear, "You belong to me now, and I do not want you to speak again tonight."

I did as I was told.

9.

The purpose of these chronicles is not to justify my actions or assign blame, and so I will not attempt to do either. I prefer that the majority of the time I spent with Les to remain unrecorded. I have pushed the details of that night from my own mind so why go through the process of remembering them here. I was neither weakened nor made stronger by this experience, it is not my defining factor, and I have seldom let it affect my life. I did what every survivor does. I pushed forward.

Upon waking after six hours of semiconscious sleep I quickly realized that my progress toward moving on was hindered by an excruciating nausea. As I lay on the bed next to my new owner I felt like every pore across my body needed to vomit. I tried to slide off the bed but only managed to collapse. The thud of my body hitting the white floor roused my bed mate and I could see his confused face peering at me from over the bed as he said, "Do you need help?" Not waiting for an answer, he stood up and lifted me by my armpits into a sitting position at the edge of the bed. None of this had helped with my body's need to purge itself. I was starting to get a bit worried, and the fact that I had to ask the pillager of my body to assist in my transportation to the toilet didn't make anything less painful.

I brought my legs towards my chest and pressed my temples into my knees. "I feel like…" A shudder pushed its way up my spine and I fell away from Les. I remained in the fetal position and continued to tremble and hope for death.

"Elinor, I do not know what you need." The big oaf actually sounded concerned. I could feel him getting up from the bed. "I will take you to Urral in the med bay. Hopefully he will be able to decipher the problem."

I felt the blanket fall on top of me and heard his body move around the room, but suddenly everything got better, and I greatly desired to do whatever I had just done again. I looked up to see Les gapping down at me and breathing much heavier than he had been a few moments before.

I gave him a lackluster smile and said, "Whatever was happening stopped. I feel quite well now actually." I rolled onto my haunches and noticed the blanket was gone. Not just pushed to the side but gone.

"Did the blanket just evaporate or something?" I turned back to Les.

"The Kara…you, " His heavy breathing was starting to become worrisome. Les no longer looked fearful for my life; he looked excited. "Somehow I have transferred the dormant Kara within my body into yours."

"There's no 'somehow' about it." I waved my arms in circular motions to encompass both of our naked bodies. "Did you give me some freaky alien disease? Have I become just another alien statistic?"

My sarcasm was lost as Les burst into action and grabbed a new blanket to cover me. "We still need to see

Urral."

His hands tightened around the pink material, and once again our faces were very close together, but something had shifted in our dynamic. "It is your own energy that feeds the Kara and pushes it to eradicate. You must warn me if you feel the need to purge again." With that he lifted me into his arms and walked out of the room. It was more of a stride than a walk, and as soon as we entered the medical area he deposited me upon a table and moved away from me before it had even fully risen from the floor.

Urral stood at the left side of the room near the wall of shelves that had long, thin tubes connecting a large screen to three humans lying on tables on the opposite side of the room. A middle-aged woman looked over at me but said nothing. The pain on their faces led me to believe that they were half way through the language assimilation process. Urral and Les had been having a hushed conversation and were making their way back to where I was perched.

"Elinor, how are you feeling?" It was Urral with his large device aimed at my head again.

"Are you really asking me or is this just small talk while your tablet scans my brain to see what's going on in there?" I was feeling snarky and in control of the situation. Whatever this Kara stuff did, confidence was a side effect.

Urral lowered the tablet and looked me in the eye. "Elinor, you have assimilated a chemical known as Kara into your system. It is a biological weapon created by the Par hundreds of years ago. It was necessary for our species to implant the serum through our spines the way we are implanting your people with our language." He leaned back as a way of acknowledging the people lying behind me. "But you… your body ingested it through the mixing of bodily fluids, and if Les is correct you have produced and purged earlier than any of our own species. This is… this is big Elinor."

A glugging sound that indicated Urral was laughing made its way into my ears, but I was far too busy trying to make sense of everything to react.

"So, I have a biological weapon inside of me." I shifted from Urral to Les but neither spoke, so I continued in my attempts at comprehension. "Is it going to hurt me or hurt anyone else?"

"Not if you are able to contain it." Urral slapped Les's back and smiled between us.

"And you are lucky enough to have an intimate relationship with the highest-level Kara soldier to ever fight in the Par ranks. If anyone can teach you how to control your Kara it is Les."

The confidence drained from my body and I was once again feeling ill. I groaned as my muscles tensed, and my companions swiftly pressed themselves against the portal on the other side of the room. A shudder of pleasure worked its way down my body, and when I opened my eyes, I could see I was engulfed by a turquoise vapor. I screamed before I comprehended that the strange mist had come from me.

Embarrassed by my overtly feminine reaction I slid off the table only to find that I had decimated the remainder of the blanket.

"Ok, so I have fire vapor seeping out of my body. Am I ever going to be able to wear clothes again?" The two cowards crept out from their hiding place behind the immobile humans and rejoined me at the front of the room.

"Are you guys going to run away every time this happens?"

Les straightened himself and strolled as nonchalantly as possible towards me. "As you must be aware, your Kara is already quite powerful. If it were to come into contact with us, we would be in the same state as the blanket. The Philex can withstand the Kara. The ship and our clothes will be unaffected. I will have Tikk find an old training suit for you to wear." Both circled me cautiously.

"It appears that it is Les that elicits the strong reaction from you." Urral glanced at Les apprehensively. "Perhaps it is best to keep her away from you until she is able to better control her Kara."

Les didn't look happy about this suggestion. “Unnecessary, creating enough energy to form the Kara is one of the main problems a fledgling soldier faces. The angrier she is the more we will have to work with. It will be fun getting to enter the training ring with real purpose again." Before anyone else could speak Tikk entered the room.

"I went to your room to inform you that we have leapt to Qualittia's atmosphere. Has something happened?" Tikk tilted his head at the scene in front of him, and I was again reminded of my nudity. "Would you like some clothes and something to eat, Elinor?" Tikk always said the right thing.

"I really would." I said as I covered as much as I could with my hands.

"Do we have any old Kara training suits left on board?" Les stepped aside as Tikk waved his hand along the back corner of the wall and a narrow shelf slide out next to a deep set drawer.

"Of course. Why are you in the med bay? Only half of the humans have received the language implant, but there have been no problems so far, right Urral." Tikk looked up searchingly.

"Elinor is here because Les has transferred the Kara to her. She now has a live Kara within her, and she has already exhibited release." Tikk stopped short as Urral spoke.

He turned to face me and said, "Elinor, this is unprecedented."

Tikk's large eyes seemed to sparkle as his smile widened. Without breaking eye contact he reached above his head and fished out a tiny black body suit. "I know you do not understand the importance of your situation right now." He handed me the garment and I stared at it cautiously. “For now, understand that something very significant for both of our species has just occurred.” At that very moment all I wanted was to get dressed and eat something. My need for food had accelerated as the conversation dragged on.

The Philex training suit covered my body ending only at the top of my neck, I was still stressed about the possibility of Kara escaping through my face. I glanced back at Les and Urral who had gotten wrapped up in their own hushed conversation over by the sleeping humans.

"Can one of you guys go and make me a… what do you call the drinks?" I looked back at Tikk hoping he was done going on about how great everything was so he could concentrate on feeding me. Finally, the glazed look left Tikk's eyes and he went into action.

“Come, I will make you something.” Tikk said as he walked towards the door.

I turned to interrupt Les and Urral before leaving. "Urral, are the humans healthy and taking well to the serum?" I had to show some form of concern for my own species.

"Yes, they are assimilating in a form rather like your own, but now this discovery of yours has made me think there could be an easier way to inject your people with the serum. If your body was able to assimilate the Kara through bodily fluids, then we may be able to transmit numerous chemicals to humans through a simple fluid exchange. Your species must be very susceptible to disease and parasites."

I could tell he was getting excited and was more than willing to discuss his new discovery for as long as I wanted, but my stomach demanded immediate attention, so I cut him short.

"It all sounds incredibly fascinating and I want to hear all about it later, but I am about to go and chug a whole liter of that meat juice."

Les had left when I interrupted his conversation with Urral, so Tikk and I made our way to the dining hall after him. I asked, "Why does my body feel like it's trying to eat itself? It obviously has something to do with this Kara thing because I would never want to drink your meat goo otherwise."

"If you have already expressed Kara then you have used a large part of your energy reserves. You will need to up your intake."

Tikk turned me into the dining room and I could see Les shoving slices of a purple meaty substance into one of the compressor machines.

"Good, I feared Urral would keep you listening to him talk about the intricacies of human anatomy indefinitely."

He opened the silver lid of the device and tossed a couple more meat chunks in before reaching for a red melon. He saw me staring at the food and attempted to endear me to his cooking. "I am making you a homp and shushu mixture. I will cook a real meal for you when we arrive at the training facilities in Sharronn. I have already had Innc inform them to prepare the arena for our arrival. It will be clean, stocked, and ready for a new army to be trained."

The buzzing of the machine stopped and Les popped the container from the bottom and held it out towards me. I took it from his hands and started gulping it down. I didn't have the energy to start asking all the questions that his statements brought up.

"This is actually pretty good." I stopped for a breath and felt the need to acknowledge Les' big expecting eyes, but I aimed the remainder of my conversation at Tikk because his face didn't make me want to punch it.

"None of them were bad really; it's just an aesthetic thing. The color and texture leaves much to be desired." I downed the rest of the contents and turned toward the large hole against the wall. "Why do you just throw these away? Why not wash and reuse them?"

Les took the container from my hand and tossed it into the Zorb hole. "We are always in need of energy to travel, but there is an endless supply of Philex on Tralccore. The ships stores are still nearly full, and we have been off planet for over seven full rotations."

I narrowed my eyes at him. "Endless supply sounds a bit too good to be true. This seems more like waste to me." Tikk stepped into my field of vision and broke the tension between possession and owner.

"We will be docking at Sharronn any moment. Elinor, you should be with your people. Obviously, everything has changed, and we will be taking them with us to the training fields instead of straight to the warehouses." Les made a grunt of agreement but Tikk continued. "Les and the rest of us need to discuss what will be done now that our plans have changed. For now, have your people ready themselves to leave. Only some will have assimilated the language serum."

I was suddenly very apprehensive about seeing my brother and the rest of my friends. I was once again set apart from them. "I assume you now plan on injecting them with this Kara thing too. How quickly we have gone from useless cattle to a critical factor."

With that I beamed at my purchaser and left the room.

10.

I am going to gloss over the clusterfuck of moving 71 frightened and confused humans from the cargo bay of the Par's ship to the training arena by instead giving a quick lesson in Par history because I know many of you didn't pay attention in school.

Qualittia is located in the galaxy known as Lorttar. The Par began exploring the universe about two hundred years before humans did. It only took them about one hundred and fifty to invent Zorb technology and make their first big discovery. The galaxy was labeled Xinggot and houses the planet Tralccore.

Tralccore, is primarily a flora planet, but with a thriving ocean environment that will hopefully develop into intelligent organisms in the next couple eons if only we would allow it to do so. One thing about Tralccore that made it so spectacular for life was what the Par lovingly labeled the Tralcaccians, a Nitrogen based life form that had a critical role in the lush Oxygen rich atmosphere of Tralccore.

Tralccore held an abundance of behemoth flora that the Par began cultivating. Philex, the versatile substance my new clothes and the Par's ship were made of, came from Tralccore. Most of the vegetation was found to be hostile to the Par's systems but there was enough Philex and other useful material on the planet for the Par to justify claiming it as their own. No Par ever set up house there due to the insanely high oxygen levels, but there has been an outpost on Tralccore with at least one troop of Par soldiers for over two hundred rotations.

Parrian corporations took over most of the exceedingly easy interactions between the Tralcaccians and Par, since the Tralcaccians had no way to communicate any grievances to their new landlords. For the few of you that have not seen them, the Tralcaccians are simple life forms that resemble yellow moss but at any given time the fuzzy yellow balls could start sparkling with a rainbow of colors. It has lately been discovered that this is how they communicate with one another, but at the time this was considered a meaningless biological reaction. The Tralcaccians are mobile and skitter around on small suction like feelers located along the bottom of their bodies. They can be as small as a human eye or as large as a full grown Par male, and reproduce through mitosis.

They didn't seem to mind when the Par came in and started stripping their plant life. It was almost like they enjoyed the extra work and oxygen excretion it took to re-cultivate their lush planet.

The second planet the Par stumbled upon is located in a galaxy the Par have labeled Valakka. The life on this planet, the Vokkna to the Par, are far more intelligent, and far more difficult to subdue. Valakarri, the planet itself, is a highly inhospitable atmosphere to the Par and humans, but the Vokkna, being a helium based life form, flourished in the thin air. I am sure all of you have seen images of the sand storms known as the Vokkna. I am also sure that many of you have allowed their otherness, their strangeness, to hinder your view of them as a species and culture. The anti-Vokkna propaganda has only recently died down. I have found that knowledge is the only cure for this kind of hate.

The Vokkna are massive creatures that live in a oligarcy and extremely violent society. Despite their appearance, the Vokkna are a highly intelligent species and brutal when it comes to protecting what they believe to be theirs. The caves of Valakarri contain a precious mineral known to the Par as boorgant, which is used to norish fields on both Qualittia and Tralccore. The Par didn't discover boorgant until many years into the Vokkna wars, but the Vokkna and all other life on the planet were considered unintelligent and unimportant in the grand scheme of things, so the Par thought it their right to do whatever they pleased. It turned out the Vokkna were willing to fight for their land, and the Par prided themselves in never stepping down when their superiority was threatened, so a war of very little ensued. Although the Par had vastly superior technology the Vokkna outnumbered them ten to one, and since the Vokkna have no body in the classic sense, fighting them was something the Par had not prepared for.

The Par quickly decided to call it quits on the planet with the unfriendly inhabitants, but they made a fatal error in judgment when they assumed that because they could not understand the new found species, the Vokkna were unintelligent. In their haste to leave, the Par abandoned two crashed turbo fighters on the planet, and within sixty years the Vokkna had created a fighting fleet of their own. Tracing Qualittia by using the coordinates found in the turbos the Vokkna counter-attacked their supposed colonizers. Since Par is not as helium rich as Valakarri, the Vokkna were unable to fragment and turned to mud as soon as they exited their ship, making them easy to defeat when on Qualittia, but a whole new pile of shit had hit the fan and the first interplanetary war had begun.

This is when the Kara that was to be introduced into my own system came into play. The Par had created the biological weapon known as the Kara within ten rotations of discovering Valakarri. The main component of the serum was found in a flower located in the oceans of Tralccore and like most great discoveries the whole thing happened by accident, and within a couple years the Par had created a weapon without an equal, and more importantly, they created a weapon that could kill a sand storm.

The Par dominated both the Vokkna and Tralcaccians for over over one hundred rotations. As their war with the Vokkna raged on they continued to search the galaxy and eventually found Hurran, home of the Harlukkna. Hurran was a planet very similar to Qualittia itself, but with one very important difference. The planet has an endless supply of tsunamis raging across its tumultuous landscape. All life on the planet developed below ground in Hurran's intricate cave system. The Harlukkna are the most intelligent of these species.

As you should all know, the Harlukkna were the first species, with a spinal cord, the Par encountered, and so despite evolving in moisture rich, darkness, the Harlukkna share many similarities with the Par and humans alike. For those that did not pay close attention in alien anatomy, the Harlukkna body is fluid and their epidermis so thin it is nearly transparent. Their spines are the only bone in their body; the rest of their limbs are formed by a flexible cartilage. They move as if they are in water, and the highly humid environment of Harrua leads to the amphibious theme.

The most drastic difference between the Harlukkna and Par is their reproductive methods. The Harlukkna use mitosis to create new life, and so they do not have two separate genders the way the Par and humans do. The Harlukkna contain both male and female organs, so they refer to themselves by individual names, or as the collective.

Many Par have the misconception of thinking the Harlukkna have large eyes that take up the entire top half of their heads. In fact, these are sensory organs. They are covered in tiny fibers and can take in both light and movement. Their three upper appendages could be compared to the arms of humans and Par, which they use to sense their environment as well as the emotional state of those around them, and their three lower tentacles, could be seen as legs that glide across the ground instead of raise to walk.

The Harlukkna were the first species to receive a dose of LiquiParian. They were chosen more for their easy demeanor, and the fact that they didn't attempt to kill any of the Par upon their first encounter, than any real desire for communication on the Par's part. Of course, the Harlukkna do not speak the way humans and Par do. Instead they project emotion and meaning by changing the shade of their skin and by gesturing with their upper limbs. Each upper limb ends with seven thinner filaments that the Harlukkna can manipulate into any shape, and so they were all equipped with translation bands that project their meaning in Par.

Once communication lines were opened and the harsh climate of Hurran was acknowledged the Par quickly formed a treaty with the intelligent and peaceful Harlukkna in order to promote trade and corporation with a planet they would have had much difficulty cultivating on their own. The Par are power hungry but not stupid, and from the history logs it is easy to glean that the Par were impressed with their newest colonists, and the species continue to cooperate in harmony today.

Of course, once the non-confrontational Harlukkna became aware of the wars raging between their new acquaintances and other alien life forms they began to push for talks towards peace. The Harlukkna even attempted to communicate with Vokkna independent of the Par. Even going as far as to send a peace committee to the planet, which only ended in more hostility, but did lead to the realization that the Harlukkna's liquid heavy bodies did not react to the Vokkna's enveloping embrace the way the Par did.

The Vokkna's fighting style of encircling their opponent and crushing them into dust particles was no match for the Harlukkna's overwhelming dampness. To defeat a Harllukna, the Vokkna had to expel most of their own energy. When the Par came into contact with a Vokkna, their dry thick skin was quickly crushed into sand, and humans, although they contained more liquid than Par, were also eventually consumed by the swirling mass of hard cartilage that made up the Vokkna anatomy.

There were Par that desired peace with the Vokkna and even worked with the Harlukkna in an attempt to establish communication with them, but it appeared as if the Vokkna had little interest in being understood by their enemies. The first official peace summit was held about one hundred rotations ago, and has been revamped every fifty. Most Par looked on this peace talk as laughable and the Vokkna never made any attempt at real communication, but the Harlukkna, who need the boorgant as much as the Par do, continued to strive for real peace, and for that perseverance I have always respected them.

Skipping over years of failed negotiations and we come to the great tragedy that put the Par in their current position. The Vokkna had learned one thing from their enemies and that was that biological warfare was key. The Kara was the only weapon that could beat the Vokkna at their own game, and the Par had placed Kara fueled shields around their entire planet and around Tralcorre so the only way for the Voknna to reach them on their own turf was to create something that could slip through the atmosphere. By analyzing dead Par soldiers the Vokkna were able to create an anti-Kara serum. A massive attack was planned and carried out during one of the peace talks. Hurran, Qualittia, and Tralcorre were hit with massive gas attacks containing a substance the Par never bothered giving a fancy name to. No one was physically injured in the attack, but the Kara became dormant in their systems. The Par's only weapon for the past twenty hundred rotations was taken from them. The Vokkna's technology grew everyday while the Par seemed to be at a standstill, and it was only a matter of time before fuel storage for the shields ran out. Of course, now the Par were more than willing to participate in peace negotiations, but the Vokkan seemed to be only too happy to take on their new role as the dominate species in the universe.

That brings us pretty much up to date. It was clear that humans now held the key to everything the Par had lost. We were the replacement for the weapon that had been taken from them, and we were about to be thrown into a war we had no reason or right to get involved in, but not being in the right never stopped us before so why it should now.

11.

"Elinor, he raped you. That fucking asshole raped you!" I was sitting on top of a cushion with Ming and Judas while Ming held my face between her hands and shook it a bit rougher than I thought necessary.

"So let me get this straight, while we got our spines ripped apart by their language serum you were fucking big and purple and getting yourself infected with some death mist that seeps out of your pores. What the fuck, El?"

Judas was giving me a look that hinged on the border of rage and annoyance. We arrived at the training arena an hour earlier and found a secluded room in the seemingly endless halls that circled the main facility. There were hundreds more rooms than necessary so, after we ensured everyone was safely in a room, we slinked off for a moment alone. I had divulged the previous night's episode to explain the minty cloud that burst from my face every fraction or so.

Mainly I had just succeeded in turning the whole scene into a judgment party. "It wasn't exactly my idea now was it?" I pulled Ming's hands from around my face but continued to hold them in my lap. "He's not the kind of guy that likes to hear no, and he weighs at least twice as much as me. I didn't want or expect this to happen, but we are here now and in reality, our options on this planet have gotten a bit better."

I rethought my statement as Ming narrowed her eyes

at me. "Maybe not better but at least they have broadened to two instead of one. We have something they want now. Even if it involves taking that Kara thing into our systems."

"Help me to understand," Judas stood and began to pace the small, white room. "He bought you and now technically owns you." Judas looked down and I just shrugged. I had already told them the story and I had no interest in repeating myself. "But now that you have this thing inside you, the tables have turned, right? He can't own someone that can easily kill him. Maybe it would be good for all of us to get a… Kara?" I nod when his questioning gaze rested on me.

"So, are we all going to have sex with one of them in order to acquire it?" Ming always focused on the important stuff. "Not that they don't have an interesting look. The pink one gets me going in a kinky sort of way." She smiled and wrapped her arm around me. I hadn't had a Kara episode since we had made it to the room.

"No way." The annoyed part of Judas' features was winning out over his anger. "I'm not going to let some alien mount me just in order to… to… what the hell do they even want us to do with this thing anyway?"

"What do you do with a biological weapon? It certainly isn't for entertainment."

I heard noise outside as people explored. The arena was massive, so I knew we would be undisturbed until Les started looking for me.

We didn't have much time to talk this morning but

all of them seemed so excited about my new parasite.

“Urral, the pink one," Ming pinched my stomach when I leaned into her and continued. "He said that the Kara is dormant in their systems so it’s definitely something they at one time used and want to use again. They are trying to turn us into an army. Why else change their plans and bring us to a training facility? They obviously want to prepare us for a fight."

"Well, the being a slave thing is starting to sound much more appealing to me. I'm a lover not a fighter." Ming raised her hands as she spoke. "You need to figure out exactly what is going to happen here. Judas is the youngest of us and he's thirty-six. Well, I guess you would count as the youngest but in years you are forty. Either way, how do they expect to make an army out of a bunch of old worn out humans that have zero idea or interest in what they are fighting for?"

"I get it." I rose to my feet. "I'll find Les and get more details. Just rest, you look like shit." I directed my last commit at Judas because his judgmental gaze was starting to piss me off.

I searched for Les in one of the halls that led from the main walk way into what had to be the training area. I stepped into the massive oval arena and surveyed the sun-drenched floor and walls. There was either no ceiling or it was a massive portal. I walked into the middle of the white room and felt my feet bounce on the matted floor. I could smell the air change and when I turned, I found Les in the opening with his usual grimace.

"Are the humans settled? We will need to begin the process of infecting them with the Kara tonight."

"Don't use the word infect around any of them. Doesn't sell it. Do you really expect all of them to... be fighters or whatever it is you are thinking? Some of them are over sixty." I turned to reexamine the large room.

"No, not all the humans will be able to accept the Kara and not all are fit to become Kara warriors, but there are at least twenty that have potential. We will begin the process of implanting them tomorrow and see how their bodies react. If yours is any indicator the humans will be a strong Kara host, and the training will be difficult but not impossible."

I kept my back to him so he wouldn't see the excitement on my face. I didn't know what my purpose was at that moment but the idea of once again doing something that mattered got my Kara pumping. I had already learned how to push it out on my body in order to quell my nausea. I turned back to see Les anxiously watching the mist pulsating from my face, and I reveled in my newfound power over him. "When do we start?"

"You and I will start now." With that he turned on his heal and left the room and returned covered with the Philex material from head to foot.

"How can you see with that on?"

"I can see." He replied. "Now, envision your hands free of the Philex," He said as he approached me. I looked towards my palms and imagined them without the Philex covering them and the material came to life. It crept away from my fingers like a living blob and came to rest smoothly on my wrists. He stood before me akimbo.

" You're not used to being the one with the suit on are you? Why is the Kara dormant in your system?" I asked, as he shifted in discomfort.

"That is a very long story for another time. The Par have been at war for over two hundred and fifty years. We are currently in serious danger of losing that war, but now that the Kara is once again available to us, we have a chance of destroying the Vokkna forever." He stepped forward and reached for me. "You now have the ability to save the Par and yourselves."

I stepped back and shrugged my shoulders. "These Vokkna guys have no issue with humans. The only reason they would ever have to label us as the enemy is if we decide to help you, and I don't know how I feel about it, let alone how the rest of the humans will."

"The Vokkna hate all races not their own. They will want to annihilate you the very same moment they learn about your existence. Especially now that you have the Kara inside of you." He placed his hands behind his head and leaned into a small back bend. "This was not in my original plan either, Elinor." He had not used my name in that way before. He was restraining himself.

"You guys won't have to have sex with everyone in order to transfer the Kara into their systems, right? You can inject them like you did with the LiqiParian, or you could probably just give them a simple shot." I took a deep breath. I could feel the Kara in the pit of my stomach.

"It will be painless." His arms swung down to his sides and hung limply as he continued. "Now that it is clear to Urral that almost any chemical compound can be introduced into the human system with an injection, this is how he will go about it. Your system is now stronger. The Kara changed it. It has improved you." He tilted his head and shook his arms out by his sides. "I can see the Kara building inside of you. Release it from your hands and aim for my abdomen." And that was exactly what I wanted to do. I took aim and pushed with all my might.

The lack of control I had over my newest bodily function became undeniable as the Kara shot forth from each of my exposed pores with no control. The energy from the effort knocked me off my feet and I found myself gazing up at Les's very satisfied looking face as I regained consciousness.

"Did you know that would happen?" I rose onto my elbows while I gave him a venomous stare, but I fear my point was lost as a wave of lightheadedness washed over me.

Les was lifting me into a sitting position. "You behaved in a very common manner. There is little control over the Kara in the beginning stages. You needed to see for yourself how little discipline you have. You must learn to manipulate your Kara, or it will become dangerous." His face was free of Philex and he was down on one knee at eye level.

"You are tired. I will make you dinner and we will retire for the night. The rest of the humans should be fed and in their sleeping chambers by now." He stood and reached his hand down to me. I had the overwhelming urge to bite him, but instead defiantly stood on my own.

"I'm not going to say no to food because I am famished, but I am not retiring with you anywhere ever again." He contorted his features into a look of exasperation.

"You belong to me, Elinor. You know this." He clutched at my arm as I maneuvered away from him. He leaned back to maintain a safe distance as small eruptions of Kara exploded from my face.

"You can't even touch me." I could feel the elation creeping up my spine as I backed away further. "I'm no more yours than the Kara is." I kept backing away and ended up bumping into the wall. I to find the opening to the hallway nearby.

"You are right." Les stopped and crossed his arms. "You have become the dominant species. You are still technically my property, but I have no physical power over you."

It was too easy, but I went along and I said, "Good! Fine, where is the food hall around here?"

Our dinner that night was made of legitimate food that was cooked in a classic, Paruvian fashion. The meat and vegetables were just as colorful and foreign to me as ever, but Les was a solid chef and his attentiveness to detail was surprising. I believe there were even attempts made on his part to learn about the inner workings of my psyche as the meal was prepared, but all that is unnecessary characterization that I have decided to keep out of the chronicle. Our discussion that night did not change my feelings toward him, and I left him shortly after my food had been ingested to find the room I had earlier claimed with Judas and Ming.

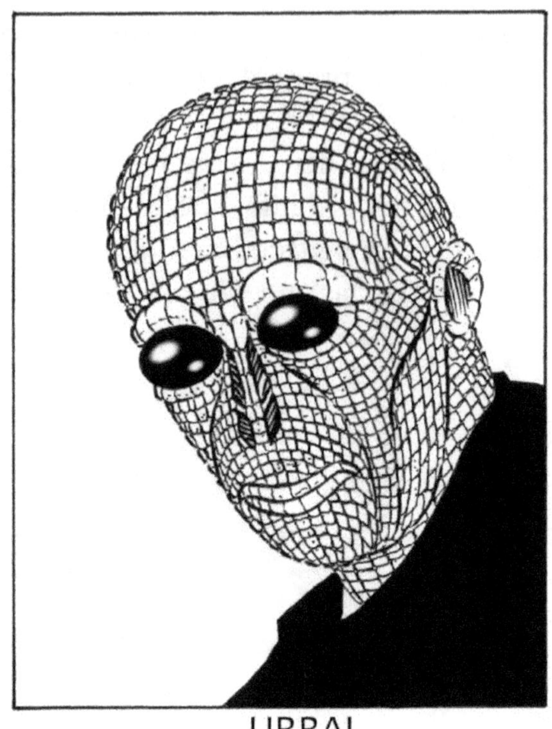
URRAL

12.

I was awoken the next morning by a piercing siren wailing through the halls of the arena. Judas' fist was punching its way up my arm as he said. "What the hell, El?"

Les and I had decided to spend the day talking with everyone and choosing who would take the Kara, who would stay on to help maintain the arena while we trained, and who would be auctioned off to help fund the training, but I didn't realize he wanted to start the day by shattering our eardrums.

"Don't you think I would have said something if I had known this was coming? This is terrible." I threw the blanket off and moved towards the door with my hands pressed to my ears. I hadn't bothered to find the facilities the previous night. I crawled into the bunk beside a naked Ming and fell asleep in my Philex suit. By the time I woke up my bladder was bursting.

"Would either of you know the direction of the nearest toilet?" I asked.

"Turn right and it's three openings down on the right." Ming had slid off her bunk and was dressing herself. "A guy named Innc showed me last night. I think all of us have had the language injection by now."

We made our way to the facility and found a line four humans deep so turned around in search of another. The wailing had finally stopped. The other humans had spread out along the first level of the arena and each had found a room of their own or with their spouse, for the few that had one. So, our attempts at privacy had proven unsatisfactory in gaining solace from a queue at the toilet. The large circular structure was similar to the ship but with the halls wrapping around a massive arena instead of leading to the main deck. The rooms lining the arena have large viewing portals on one wall just like the rooms on the ship, and of course the entire building was made of Philex. The beds, toilets, and cooking supplies were all tucked away like on the ship and there were no doors. People were having difficulty adjusting but we did our best to look straight forward when walking along the halls.

Every fifth doorway along the hall led to a facility and so Judas, Ming, and I made our way to find a toilet without a line. The arena is six stories high and has two wide spiral stairs set on opposite sides of the building. We discovered these stairs in our search for a facility and took them to the second floor which was currently empty.

The Par had taken over the top level of the arena where the dining hall and lounge area were located. All the humans, myself included, were not aware of this yet and so my two fellow adventures and I settled on the three nearest facilities on the second floor.

I was the first to exit so I began to look around the other rooms and found them to be identical to the ones below.

As my brother came into the hallway, I asked him, "Do you want to come up here tonight? Get the place to ourselves." I spread out my arms as Ming joined us smiling. They were both wearing Philex body suits by this time.

"I'd be fine with that." Judas said walking toward the stairs. "Where are we supposed to go?" He turned to look at me as he spoke.

I could hear Urral's disembodied voice asking everyone to meet in the main arena, so we ran downstairs to join the others. I saw Tikk, Innc, and Urral towering over a growing group of humans when I turned into the large padded room. I didn't have to scan the crowd to know Les wasn't there. I caught Tikk's eye and meandered toward him as the last people trickled in. The air was tense.

"Where is Les?" I asked.

"Obtaining supplies. He does not need to be here for this." Tikk replied as he faced the rest of the crowd. His voice became formal and sharp as he addressed them. "We have created a list of humans that are to be auctioned off in order to fund our training efforts. If you hear your name, please break off from the group and move toward the back of the arena." Tikk's arm rose to indicate the area of the room behind us, but before he could start again the crowd broke into murmurs.

"You're just going to sell us off like animals!" It was an old man I did not know.

"You are animals." Was Tikk's response.

I could see the confusion in Tikk's face as he made a statement, he clearly thought was obvious. They apparently hadn't expected to be met with hostility.

"Now you must settle yourselves so that my voice can be heard." He was holding on of the clear tablets which he focused his gaze on.

"Did you know about this?" Judas' eyes flared with rage. He had made his way to where I stood with Tikk and he pushed Tikk's large green shoulder as he continued. "You don't get to just sell us. We don't belong to you, asshole." Judas attempted to pull the tablet from Tikk's grasp but only succeeded in getting everyone riled up.

Innc had Judas' arms behind his back before anyone could move and Tikk raised his arms in a plea for quiet.

"Please, we do not wish to create tensions," Tikk said raising his head to look at the entire crowd. "You must understand that you do belong to us."

Tikk lowered his arms and nodded to Innc who released Judas. Tikk sighed heavily and placed his hand on my brother's shoulder. The massive green hand strained as if the Par male could barely support himself. Judas leaned into the pressure and was forced to step back to support the weight.

Tikk continued in a whisper. "We saved you from a dead planet. You are an inferior species. You cannot deny your situation. Do not cause us to get physical. You are worth much less to us dead."

With that forty-eight names were perfectly enunciated by the alien's tongue. There were no more cries of outrage. The air became complacent at the mention of physical action. Everyone under fifty was staying while the rest were sold.

"Thank you for your cooperation," Tikk said as he and Innc made their way to the back of the room. "Innc will load you onto a carrier craft and you will be taken to the auction facility. Do not be afraid. You will be clothed, fed, and housed. You will one day understand the significance of your sacrifice."

"And so, what is our purpose here? To slave away our

remaining years and die in a strange place?" A small, dark woman said this as if she were making a comment about the mild weather.

"The money we make from your sale will fund the army that will destroy the Vokkna and save us all." Tikk was again confused by the fact that these people did not see the merit in the Par's plan.

"And humanity will carry on," Urral added with his hands behind his back as Innc made his way to the exit. "Not as it is now but a new species will be created, and adaptation is the answer to true survival." His finger had shot into the air, and he was so proud of his little speech that I couldn't bear to tell him that everyone in the left corner of the room hated his guts at that moment. People stared at him outraged as they began to file out of the room with encouragement from Innc.

I slid up to Urral's side and whispered. "Just leave it. They are totally justified in being pissed and telling them humanity as they know it is finished will not help them get over it." I said to his disgruntled face.

"They should be proud of the contribution they are making to the war." He looked after the last of the people leaving the arena. "I know they don't understand now, but they couldn't help any other way."

"Are you guys going to explain everything to the rest of us at least?" I motioned toward the twenty-four humans standing behind me.

Judas and Ming were the only members of the crowd that I knew. The man, Luke, who had questioned the

Par's motives back on Kepler stood in the front looking pompous as ever, but other than that I was just as much a stranger to them as Tikk and Urral.

I answered Urral's flummoxed look with a shrug and said, "I'm just as familiar with these people as you are. You really choose the wrong ambassador in me."

I linked my arm with his and we approached the unfriendly looking group together. I released Urral to join my fellow, soon to be, Kara warriors.

"Ok gentlemen, it's your show. Tell us what we are doing here."

Tikk took an awkward step into the center of the arena and glanced around before beginning. "Yes, to the task at hand."

Again, he inclined his head towards the entrance behind us. "As I am sure some of you are aware, Elinor has been exposed to a chemical weapon called Kara. The Kara is a… compound that works with your system… Do you want to do this part Urral?" Tikk pleadingly turned to Urral.

"Yes, of course." Urral burst into action. "That is my part isn't it?"

They both began fumbling with their tablets. "As Tikk said, the Kara is a chemical weapon that links into the nervous, lymphatic, and immune systems."

A hologram burst into life behind the two aliens. I could make out the outline of the human anatomy, but all the mathematical equations and chemical compounds were lost on me.

"Of course, this is after it has been transferred through… well we will be attempting to give you a simple injection."

With a pleading look at me he waved his hand at the diagram as if to indicate something. Tikk appeared just as confused as the rest of us.

"Uhh, the Kara has been a part of Par's culture for hundreds of years, but for the past twenty it has rested in our systems dormant."

The long silences were getting brutal. As the two of them floundered with their devices it became obvious just how little these guys dealt with personal relations. The very thought of them trying to create this presentation brought a smile to my face, but that wasn't going to give me the Kara build up I needed so I thought of Les instead. That did it.

"Hey guys, check this out." As the nauseous feeling built, I ran to the empty area opposite of where we stood and pushed the Kara from my body. My only thought had been to not hit any of them, and to my delight the emerald mist erupted from my hands and shot in nearly every direction, other than theirs.

"That's why you kept running off all suspiciously. We all thought you were pregnant or were helping the aliens plot against us." A woman with short black hair exclaimed from the back.

"Well that's kind of lame of you guys, but yes I have

been behaving a bit strange and it's because of the Kara." I bounced on my toes as I waited for more questions.

"I'm assuming you intend to inject all of us with that, but then what? We put on a floor show." Luke spoke up in the same condescending tone as before.

"As you can see, Elinor was sure to get away from the group before releasing her Kara." Urral started circling us. "That is because the Kara is lethal. It is made up of a chemical compound that breaks down all matter upon contact. The Kara will spread and eat up all biological matter connected to its place of contact. Kara only kills, never maims. So, we will begin training without the Kara at first. Some of you will not qualify for the injection. There are any number of physical and psychological reasons why a... human will not qualify, but that does not mean you will not be useful to the war cause."

Urral was in his zone now. "We will start out with a simple physical exam today. Perhaps it would be best to eat and get acquainted with the arena first." He stopped short as he reached Tikk.

"Are you hungry?" He was facing Tikk, but it was projected as a question to the room.

"Famished." Judas had his arms crossed tightly across his chest, but I could tell he was excited. "How about you fill us in on this "war" while you make us something to eat." He seriously made the air quotes.

"Of course. Runn is an excellent cook, and food will help everyone maintain a sense of calm. Please follow me," Urral said as he moved toward the exit with Tikk close on his heels. I lifted my eyebrow in Judas' direction then followed.

"Les should be joining us soon. He is at the market making purchases necessary to restock the arena." Tikk spoke over his left shoulder as we made our way down the hall. "He will be the best at explaining procedures and tactics. Urral and I are scientists really."

He nudged his friend in the ribs and they both gurgled out a laugh. The rest of us remained quiet and confused. Noticing our silence Tikk continued. "We are not the best for explaining how you will use your Kara but Les wanted us to be here to answer any health questions that may arise. Actually, Runn will be able to answer any combat questions you may have."

We reached the top of the stairs and entered the elaborate kitchen where Les had made me dinner the night before. Like all the others, this room was pristine white with large black heating slabs in both corners. The two giant slabs of Qualittia steal could press a chunk of juwwakon meat into delicious medium rare in less than ten seconds. Les had made us a couple of bright purple Hommp steaks for our dinner and so I got the full demonstration.

Philex countertops circled the room and the center was dominated by a long freezer. The top could slide to the right or left to access the produce and protein that resided inside. This food receptacle was mostly empty, but as promised Runn stood in the middle of the room facing the back wall and the large baking box that was located there. This oven was long and slid open from the top in a similar fashion to the fridge. I was too intimidated by all the big hot surfaces to touch anything

Runn turned to face us. "You can help prepare the shusshu and bott. Slide the cooler's cover to the right and you will see some large red spheres, those are the shusshu, and next to it should be a green leafy plant, that is the bott." All twenty- four of us fit easily around the large cooler, and two men that were closest to the right side began their search.

"Tonight, we will learn how to make a basic Par meal, Juwwakon beast with raw shusshu and bott." Tikk and Urral flanked the exit and watched the spectacle of their new warriors' first cooking lesson.

13.

The huge cooler moonlighted as an informal table, so our band of misfits placed the large breast of juwwakon beast on a serving tray next to the sliced shusshu and bott and dug in. Just as on the ship, water faucets were in every room and jars were passed out as the food was dispersed.

"Everyone should keep a container with them at all times." Urral lectured as we began to eat. "Your biology requires much more liquid than ours. The climate of Qualittia is dry and you are all quite wet."

Ming and I giggled at this statement as I used the bott to make a wrap out of the Juwwakon and shusshu. I was very pleased with my decision to do so and chose shusshu as my new favorite food. Tikk had taken on the role of meat carver and we started to get a bit grabby by the time Les entered the room.

We tried to focus on more biological questions, but the main topic of conversation was our curiosity about the coming battle. By this point everyone knew how the Kara worked, how they would inject it into our systems, who the Vokkna were, and had come to realize that we were now expected to kill all the bad guys.

Runn was the only one in the room who had come face to face with the Vokkna, but he had only seen three years of battle, before the anti-serum, and was much more knowledgeable about the training process than the actual battle field. As Les entered the room I could feel everyone hold their breath.

"I am glad to see you enjoying the juwwakon. Has everything been discussed?" Les leaned in between Tikk and myself to grab a piece of meat.

The small, dark haired woman's hand shot into the air before anyone could respond. Les and the other three Par males stared at her in complete bewilderment. "Are you trying to communicate something to us?" Les looked at me and I had to squelch up my face not to laugh. I leaned over the cooler so I could make eye contact with the woman that was separated from me by a line of humans.

"I don't know your name," I said to her"

She lowered her hand and mirrored my body language. "Adeline. I wanted to discuss their training plans some more now that he's here. You're in charge, right?" She directed her attention at Les and continued, "I'm not exactly in great shape, and I'm all for helping you guys, it's actually nice to have something legitimate to do, but the truth is that I'm not going to be up for any kind of real physical competition for at least a couple months. I mean look at you guys." She waved her hand at the four colorful muscular specimens at my end of the table. I couldn't blame her. I considered myself in good physical health, but I would never be as jacked as the Par.

"I'm with her," I said and stepped away from the cooler to lean against the counter, half to see everyone and half as a way to get away from Les. "How long are you planning on training us before you expect us to fight?" Les fidgeted as the room's attention centered on him.

"I have considered this."

He turned to face me, which left his back to most of the room.

"You will not be forced to fight before you are prepared. I have planned for six months of training." He addressed everyone. "Our shields will hold the Vokkna forces at bay for at least another five years, but I want our new army to be ready by the next peace summit at Hurran." Tikk placed his hand on Les' shoulder and turned him so all I could see was his magenta back flexing with excitement.

"You are planning on attacking during the peace summit?" Tikk leaned into Les as he spoke in an attempt at privacy.

"We will discuss our strategy later. For now, we train."

With that Les made himself a wrap exactly like the one I claimed to have invented moments earlier.

"I suggest you all retire early this evening," he said as he made for the door. "We will begin training in exactly ten hours, and you will very likely have muscular pain for the next few days."

He smiled and left the room. I took a step towards the exit but stopped short when Judas took hold of my arm.

"Why are you following him?" He said, but I could tell he had already assumed my motivation.

I pulled myself free from his grip and said, "I want to ask him something." We gave each other identically annoyed looks.

"I'll be right back," I said. I exited and spotted Les leaning against the wall nearby. I cocked my head and asked, "Are you waiting for me?"

"Of course," He said as he gobbled down the last of the Juwwakon. He used the wall as a napkin as he pushed himself to standing. I could make out a brown smudge across the white surface.

"That's disgusting." I crossed my arms and indicated the area of concern with my chin.

"It will be absorbed by the Philex. Would you prefer I wipe the grease on myself?" I had already lost control of the conversation.

"Your actions make no difference to me." Now I was just lying. "When will you be infecting them with the serum?" I motioned back towards the kitchen.

"I thought we had agreed to refrain from that word. Everything depends on the physical exams today. Why don't we have this conversation in my chambers? I am sure they are far superior to those you share with your brother." He took several steps back towards the staircase.

"There is no reason for me to ever enter your chambers." My muscles flexed as I reminded myself of my power over him. "We can talk here."

"As you wish." He returned to his leaning posture and

I noticed the brown spot had faded.

"Urral and his team will analyze each human to insure their system can handle the Kara. We do not wish to harm anyone unnecessarily. If they are fit, they will be injected with the serum and hopefully it will be fully assimilated by tomorrow morning." I looked past him as he spoke, so when he finished, he was forced to change the location of his head in order to make eye contact with me.

"I will need your help during the training process. I can already see that you have a great amount of control over your Kara, and that you are in far superior physical condition compared to your comrades. You can feel the Kara welling inside of you even now, can you not?"

Of course, he was right. The longer I stood near him the more nauseous I felt, but I was able to control my release better than before.

"I can feel it but it's a different sensation, like I'm in control instead of it being in control." I shrugged and stepped away from him. "You know I'll do whatever you guys need. Despite the insanity of the past couple of days, you guys are our saviors. You ensured the survival of our species and we are indebted to you." I smiled and began walking backwards. He did not attempt to follow me. "Try and remember, we all feel that way because we are most likely going to be a bunch of assholes for the next few lunations."

With that I turned back to the kitchen.

14.

Urral wanted to start the examination process with the youngest and most physically fit specimens first and then work his way down the list ending with me since I already had the Kara. I got bored after the first exam. Everything was automatic and so I was left with plenty of time to talk to Urral about my new-found home.

"When will we get to explore Qualittia and meet the rest of the population? They do know we're here, right?"

I was perched on a table near the viewing portal in the large medical bay located on the top floor of the arena. The view was magnificent. Qualittia was primarily made up of dark sand, from what I could make out, and the large city of Sharronn was a freckling of white across the nearly black landscape. Greenery speckled the land as well and was primarily in the form of spikey bushes and tall, thin trees with foliage at the top. I was unable to take my eyes from the black landscape that sparkled in the sunlight. Judas was having the same difficulty as he prepared for his injection.

Urral said, "The Par know your people have arrived and we are in the process of organizing a banquet to introduce you to the population and explain our plans to the leading governors. The humans that were auctioned off were the Par's first interaction with your species and everything went smoothly from what I hear from Innc."

Urral did not take his eyes from his many screens and so did not notice our obsession with the world outside the arena.

"These tablets are very similar to ours." Judas stood before Urral as the pink alien scanned him and the screen behind me started to beep and light up with images of Judas' insides. Judas arched his neck to see what was on the tablet that Urral held and Urral leaned backward with a grunt.

"Please remain still." Urral lightly pushed Judas back to his position and continued. "If you wish to have an explanation of our technology, I'm sure Tikk would be more than happy to educate you, but for now please remain as still as possible and place your hands by your sides." Judas let his arms hang and gave me a smirk.

"So, we're getting a banquet, huh? I bet you guys are pretty excited to have found us."

Judas was starting to shift from one leg to the other as he puffed out his chest.

Urral lowered the tablet and said, "We were on the verge of destruction, so yes, the populace will be pleased to hear there is new hope in the war against the Vokkna, but I personally am not happy for the renewal of war. You are finished." His pink hand waved in a dismissive way and he locked eyes with Bryyl, a dark blue behemoth, and said, "He is a go for the serum." Bryyl had somehow been wrangled into being Urral's assistant for the day, but from what I could see he was just as uncomfortable in the medical lab as I was.

"Bryyl will inject you, and then you should return to your chamber and rest." Urral said to Judas then looked toward the line of humans along the wall of the room. There were no chairs, everyone was sitting cross legged on the floor in awkward groupings.

"Whomever would like to go next can please do so." Urral seemed as bored as I was. Judas gave me a nervous side glance then hopped up on the table beside Bryyl.

Bryyl approached him from the opposite side with a short, thin tube in his right hand. He rested his other hand on Judas' back and made his best attempt at a smile, but only managing to bare his teeth. "I will inject you with the Kara serum now. It should not hurt, but you are the first human to be injected so you will have to inform us of the sensation."

"Well, that certainly, fuck!" Bryyl had jabbed one end of the cylinder against Judas' neck as he had been speaking.

"Yea, it hurts. Hurts a hell of a lot." Judas slid off the table and held the side of his neck where the injection had occurred.

"Allow me to view the injection site." Bryyl moved Judas' hand and ran his finger across the tiny red hole that had been created. "It appears well. Please return to your chambers and rest until it is time for nourishment." Judas turned to me as he headed for the exit, and his place was taken by Bo, a man that had just been informed he was also eligible for the serum.

"You want to come keep me company, El?" Judas said then turned to Bryyl. "Do you guys have any kind of entertainment? Books, video, or do you just sit around practicing intimidating glares in your free time?" I couldn't help but laugh as I watched the look of confusion spread across Bryyl's face.

"Oh, damn dude!" Bo exclaimed as he flinched away from the silver device in Bryyl's hand that had just punctured his neck.

"We have many volumes of reading material and holographic videos for entertainment in the lounge."

Bryyl was annoyed with the agonized Bo and he pushed him off the table as he said, "you should have been prepared for the pain." Bryyl and Bo glared at each other with misunderstanding clouding their eyes. "Your comrade stated that the injection hurt."

Bo slinked off to stand behind Judas and a woman named Alva took his place on the table next to me. The line was moving now, and Ming was in the process of trying to flirt with Urral while he conducted the exam.

"Will you be joining us for dinner tonight?" She asked as he fiddled with the tablet and did not look at her. "I really love you guys' food, but anything new gets me excited."

She gave me a flabbergasted look. Urral was not behaving in the manner she wanted.

"Do you have restaurants and things like that, or do you do all your cooking at home?" She rested her fingers on the top of the tablet, which broke Urral's concentration and caused him to look at her.

"I apologize. I was not listening to you. You were

talking about food, correct? We will eat again in a few fractions, or you may go to the dining hall and prepare something yourself, but I recommend rest right after the injection, which you are qualified for." He smiled and waved his hand in the same manner he had done to Alva, Judas, and Bo.

I suppressed a giggle at Ming's hurt expression and said, "You'll be at dinner right Urral? Ming and I want to talk with you about the banquet you mentioned."

I watched while Alva was silently injected. She smiled at Bryyl's approving look and stuck her tongue out at Bo.

"Yes, I suppose I will have time to eat with the group, and since we are going to be a real crew again, we should start acting as such. I shall see you for dinner, but now you should all rest." Urral turned to the remaining humans and one named Ida stepped forward.

"Where's the lounge?" Bo asked as the growing group of injected humans crowded around the exit.

"On the other side of the dining hall. The entertainment is in drawers along the right wall."

Bryyl demonstrated as he spoke. "Wave your hand in a downward motion and the drawers will open. You can take anything that strikes you, but I would recommend Shallaktuyerna 5879: Across the Skies. It is one of my favorite literary series about space travel." As he spoke Bryyl drove the injector into Ming's neck and she made the slightest of squeaks. I was starting to think he was enjoying himself, but anyone that makes literature suggestions is fine in my book.

"Thanks. Do we need to get a device to make the holograms play?" I was intending on reading the book he recommended but knew reading was not Judas' thing.

"No, everything is on its own device. You will see when the drawers open. It should all be self-explanatory but if you need help you can return."

I could tell the Par were growing weary of having to explain everything to us. They had colonized before but never had to share their own planet with another species. I turned and left the room before anyone else tried to ask a question.

I entered the lounge with Bo, Judas, Ming, and Alva on my heels. We shuffled into the empty room and I made my way to the wall. This room did have one defining factor that set it apart from all the others. A large circular dent was in the middle of the floor. The indention turned out to be padded and extremely comfortable; we dove in and rolled around having a grand old time for a few moments before I moved toward the wall and waved my hand as I had seen many Par do before. Four drawers slid out of the bottom part of the wall in a vertical line. Each was filled with fifty neatly lined tablets identical to the one Urral carried with him, but each of these had indented lettering along the side that identified them. I pick out the one marked, Shallaktuyerna 5879: Across the Skies Volume I. The tablets appeared to be in alphabetical order.

I turned to the six people lying in the soft crater and said," They're all labeled. I don't know if we'll really be able to understand the plots, but it's probably a good idea to start learning about their culture and stuff." I stood and raised my new find above my head.

"I'm reading the one Bryyl suggested. I'm going to head to my chambers." I shot Judas a smile and hiked my thumb over my shoulder. "Let me know if you find a hologram and how it works. You guys should really get some rest."

"I actually don't feel tired at all." Alva had spoken up as she approached the open drawers. "I feel awake. Vibrant even. I'm starting to get excited about this stuff."

We all wore Philex training suits by then. Adeline touched her face and turned to where I watched her from the exit. "Should we keep a distance from each other?" She looked around the room apprehensively and I stepped forward to reassure her.

"You'll feel it when the Kara builds up inside of you. You'll feel sick; almost like you need to puke."

I crinkled my nose and Adeline mirrored me.

"That's when you need to get away from everyone. I think if we communicate things will be fine. You build up Kara when you are stressed or agitated; as long as everyone stays calm, we will be fine, but I still suggest everyone get some rest." I nodded at the silent stares and left the room.

15.

A few fractions later Ming leaned into my room while knocking on the side of the wall. When I glance up from the tablet laid across my lap she said, "Runn has informed me that dinner is going to be served soon." She entered the room and continued, "Actually he said, 'I am preparing nutrients for all the humans, and they will be served within the next fraction.' So, I thought I'd come get you so we can get a seat next to Urral." She pulled me to standing and bounced up and down.

"Damn girl." I laughed tossing the tablet onto my bed and taking hold of both of Ming's forearms. "You have a serious boner for Urral, you sex crazed beast." Ming pushed me away and ran her hands through her jaw length black hair.

"Oh please, I get a boner when a warm breeze wafts past." We both laugh at this as we linked arms and made our way upstairs to the kitchen.

"I'm just interested in all of them, and you seem to get along with him, the green one, Tikk, too. I guess it feels safer starting with the ones I've seen you interact with. Easier, and Urral is big and pink and I just want to snuggle with him on the big soft crater in the lounge."

We started up the stairs and Ming asked, "How's the book Bryyl suggested? We ended up playing around with the holograms.... It doesn't even feel like I'm using a foreign language."

She cocked her head at me.

"Yeah, I know. There were parts of the book that obviously were not translating exactly but I get the general idea and I like the overall plot. It's a biography of this Shalla guy and all his travels with the original space exploration team. I want to find some historical documents or something to fact check everything, and to look up some of the references I missed." We had reached the top of the stairs by this point.

"You're such a nerd, El, you are the only person I know who would arrive on an alien planet then shut themselves up alone in a room to read." Ming laughed as we entered the kitchen and found leaning room along the counter lining the outer walls.

"That's easy to say." I poked her in the side and arched my neck to try and get a look at what Runn was laying out on the freezer.

"I bet there used to be tons of humans that preferred their own company to others. There just aren't many of us left now so it's easy to be unique."

"You're probably right, but due to the fact that there are so few of us maybe you can finally make an effort to learn everyone's name; starting with Alva here."

The dark-complexioned woman with long braided hair had just leaned against the counter near us.

"Alva, you know Elinor, right?" Ming motioned between us.

"Yes, it would be difficult to not know Elinor by this

time."

Alva had a soft, deep voice that melted through me. She was in her late thirties like Judas, but her large dark brown eyes and smooth almond skin gave her the look of a much younger woman. I told myself to make the best attempt at being normal as possible, and so I reached my hand out to shake hers.

"I remember you from earlier today. You were very brave to step forward so early, and you made Bo look like a right ass in front of Bryyl."

We all smiled at each other as Ming indicated where Bo and Judas stood on the other side of the room behind Runn. They seemed to be in the process of helping Runn chop up some bright red leafs, and Runn was beginning to look annoyed at their lack of progress.

Urral entered the room with Bryyl, approached the long fridge, and began to talk with Runn.

"Let's make our move." Ming's eyes widened and Alva's eyebrows furrowed.

"Who are you planning to make a move on?" Alva searched the room.

"Are you talking about the aliens? Elinor, I have to know, are you… with the big purple one… Les?" Her eyes had rested on Urral and Bryyl as she spoke.

"No," I spat out the word before I could calm my voice. "But I'm sure it's obvious that something happened between us, and it did, but it's done." I gave her a weak smile to re-lighten the mood. "I guess it's best to get everything out in the open."

I angled myself so my back was toward the three colorful creatures and told the two women what Tikk had said about our two species breeding.

"When it comes down to it, these guys are the only chance we have a legitimate population growth. I mean, there are plenty of us to get started, but not enough to avoid any... inbreeding or crap like that. The main issue is the Par are treating us like an endangered species and it all seems so damn scientific." I shifted to look over my shoulder and caught Urral's eye. He smiled and pointed at the large purple chunk of Juwwakon beast and Alva said, "Was Les very… scientific… with you?" She was trying to be delicate, which made me want to be blunt.

"He was forceful and didn't give a shit about what I said or felt."

I looked from Ming to Alva and saw the fear in their eyes. "As far as I can tell, sex is a one-sided thing in the Par culture, but the situation Les and I were in isn't the situation anymore."

I grabbed them and pulled them in and lowered my voice. "We have the power now. They can't do anything we don't want them to." As I spoke my skin rippled and an image of Les came into my mind.

"You're right." Ming followed my lead by leaning in and lowering her voice. "We have the Kara now, not them. After we get these assholes to train us, we could take over the whole damn planet it we wanted to." She gave the nervous looking Alva a big grin. "You in?"

"I just want to… "Alva paused and looked past me. I turned to find Urral watching us.

"Are you ladies discussing something you shouldn't be?" Urral showed his massive grin again and said, "Because, if so, please join us. We are discussing the banquet that has just been announced and the topic bores me to tears."

"We were just saying that after you guys train us, we're going to take over your planet, but I would actually love to hear about the banquet."

I giggled at the shocked faces that met my statement, and then rolled my eyes.

"Come on guys that won't be for at least another rotation right." I smacked Ming's arm and pulled Alva towards the table with me.

"Is a banquet a big fancy dinner where everyone dresses up and pretends to be nice to each other? Because that's what a banquet means in our culture," Ming asked as we approached.

"That is actually a very accurate depiction of a banquet." Runn laughed as he began to cut into the Juwwakon beast. "It is a time for governors and wealthy business owners to come and examine you. To make sure you are worth all the money we are requesting of them."

"Sounds about right." Ming slid between Urral and me. "Your dad used to have one of every week it seemed like." She wrapped her arm around me.

"He did. They were the worst." I leaned my head on

her shoulder and watched Runn cut the meat. "Where are Les, and Tikk," I added as I raised my head?

"They are meeting with Rallun, the governor of our quadrant. Les usually sends one of the crew to handle diplomatic things like this but he insisted on taking care of the arrangements himself this time."

Urral nudged me and said, "I believe he finds this cause to be exceptionally important."

I ignored his last comment and pushed ahead.

"When is it? Will we all be invited?"

"Yes, of course." Bryyl spoke up as he eyed the ripped apart red leaves Bo was pilling onto a plate.

"You are the whole reason for the gathering. We are introducing you to the Par and announcing our plans for renewed war with the Vokkna." Bryyl turned abruptly to face us and focused on Alva. "Alva, I was very impressed with you today. Would you accompany me to the banquet as my partner?"

Alva, Ming and I were silent for a moment. Par males are the most aloofly forward males I had ever met. "I mean, yes that would be nice. Thank you. Bo wasn't a hard act to follow." Alva smiled and looked at her feet. If we had all been in an ancient Earth entertaining hologram this would be adorable.

"Well, Urral, are you going to ask me to be your date to the shindig, or are you already going with someone?" Ming placed her hands on her hips and jutted out her chin. "Careful how you answer. I have Kara inside these veins and I'm not afraid to use it."

"That is technically not how Kara works, but I would still be happy to accompany you to the banquet." Urral lowered his head in a partial bow and then met Ming's eyes again. "It is seen as rude for a female to be so forward with a male, but our cultures have already proven to be very different so I will assume this is common place in your society. I am very interested in what else I will discover about you during our evening together." Ming started to laugh hysterically at that.

"Elinor was right when she said you guys were all science." She smacked Urrals back, which caused him to jump. "I'll teach you some non-intellectual subjects, Urral, we'll have fun."

"The purpose of this banquet is funding, not fun." Les had entered the dining hall without anyone seeing him. He caught my eye and smiled. "But I believe we will be able to enjoy ourselves just the same, don't you?"

I admired his persistence but my disdain for him held out for a while longer. "I am glad to see you all together." Les scanned the large room filled with the 24 humans and the three Par men, "A sense of belonging is important during time of war." He lowered his head to meet my eyes and spoke quietly. "Have you already acquired an escort to the banquet?"

"I was considering asking Tikk." I looked anywhere but at Les. I had already been abandoned by my supposed comrades who had inched along the table to a place out of ear shot.

Les grinned and leaned back in a show of confidence before saying, "Tikk has his eye on another actually." He came back in even closer and inclined his head behind me at a group of four men standing at the far side of the kitchen.

"The one with the markings along his legs has captured Tikk's thoughts, and he plans on asking him for his company sometime within the next couple turns."

He was refereeing to Kang, Bo and Alva's brother. I couldn't help but cross my fingers for Tikk. I had zero idea about anyone's sexual preferences but my own. Les must have been working out because he smelled more lovely than usual. I stepped back and sighed trying to get the smell out of my head, but that just motivated Les to move in closer and take hold of my arm.

"Are you feeling faint?" There was legitimate worry in his voice.

I looked up to meet his gaze and said, "I'm fine. Have you been working out or something? You smell musky." I placed my hands on his chest and gave a little push.

He allowed me to push him back and shot me a perplexed look. "I was unloading the supplies Tikk and I purchased today and had no time to cleanse myself before my meeting with the quadrant elder." His features all curved upwards and he grabbed both of my shoulders. "Elinor, I can also smell your scent, and it entices me." He pulled me into his body, and I looked around the room.

"Great, we can smell each other." I pushed him away.

His smell was making me tense up.

"Well," I awkwardly scratched at the back of my head and then picked at the food in front of me. I had been starving but suddenly lost my appetite. I wanted to be alone in my room again. I grabbed the mostly empty plate of red leaves and started placing sliced Juwwakon onto it and spoke without any real thought to what I was saying.

"Since we seem to be the losers without dates, I guess we might as well go together, huh?" I glanced at him and gave my best I-don't-care-if-you-don't-care shrug. "I mean, stick with the evil you know and if you piss me off I'll just evaporate you."

I had finished making my plate and was ready to retreat into my cave until the next morning. I turned to leave and Les moved to block my path.

"You continue to surprise me, Elinor, and I enjoy this." Now he looked like the awkward one. "The banquet will be held on the first day of the new lunation." Upon seeing my confused look, he continued, "Which is twenty-eight turns from now. Plenty of time to prepare you for the cultural differences between our species, and to find you the proper attire." He seemed to finally notice the plate of food in my hand. "Are you taking your nutrients to your room? I can assist you or carry your liquid." He reached out for the containers in my hands.

"Thanks, I got it, really." We were in the middle of a strange dance and I maneuvered around him and out the archway. "I would prefer to spend some time alone. I'm not accustomed to so many other.... living things being around me, but thanks." I started to back away. "Will we begin training tomorrow?"

"Yes, the alarm will sound, and we will first meet here for a light meal. Then your training will begin." He crossed his arms and watched me as I slowly backed away.

"Good," I nodded. "Till then." I turned and moved toward the stairs.

"Rest well, Elinor." Les spoke as he watched me descend. His smell did not leave me the whole night and try as I might I could not concentrate on my text.

MING

16.

As promised, training started the next day, and it was brutal. I considered myself a healthy person and I had maintained a weight and cardio regiment throughout my time as a Searcher, but nothing had prepared me for the kind of training the Par had in store for us. The rest of the newly implanted Kara warriors were even worse off than me. I'm going to montage our way through the first lunation of training because it was a bit embarrassing.

We were a classic ragtag band of unprepared and

unwilling recruits in the hands of overly serious and overly pumped up coaches. The Par were not interested in how much our bodies ached, or our stomachs writhed in pain. They pushed us to the brink and continuously shoved Yurrlu down our throats to keep us going. Les claimed the thick Yurrlu drink was the best and quickest way to take in nutrients and, since that was what we would be consuming while on our mission, we should also train with it. It had become my norm to drink seven of these a day, but I eventually began to crave Juwwakon beast and shushu fruit like mad. My hunger grew every day and although everyone was consuming more food to sustain their Kara, I seemed to be eating two times as much as my fellow trainees.

The Par were primarily focused on cardio training in the beginning but after about ten turns we integrated the huge round weights into the work-out for at least two fractions a day. Tikk said running was primary because we would need to be able to cut through a defense with the Kara and then get the hell out of the way when our reserves were depleted.

Every turn started with a run followed by weight training and then strategy training, which usually consisted of three fractions of discussion-based learning and time to read up on past battle logs. The Par were big on formations and working as a group. This was also the time we spent planning our first attack scheduled for the coming peace summit. Around midday we did a series of sprint intervals followed by Kara training, which was always my favorite part of the day.

Our first day of Kara training was laughable, but telling, in our individual development as Kara warriors. Only eleven of those receiving the injection exhibited the Kara by the next morning. The people that didn't were moved into care positions around the arena. I remember hearing a deep sigh of relief from Ming's cousin, Mei, when she was scanned by Urral and came out negative. The humans immediately took over the roles of cooks, maintenance, and Urral had Ya and Nuria begin training as medical assistants.

This shift made it possible for the Par warriors to take part in our training while humans took over the grunt work of maintaining the arena, which meant we now had one on one, former Kara warrior, training partners. Our Kara warrior squadron consisted of Ming, Judas, Bo, Alva, Kang, Luke, Ansely, Talbot, Adeline, Odelia, and me. We were the definition of ragtag. I was a fast study and moments into the first official day of training I was able to focus in on a specific part of Les' body.

He even took his Philex mask off as he said, "You need to focus both on the place on your body that you wish to release the Kara, as well as the place on my body you wish to hit."

We stood apart from the rest of the group, having separated into pairs, and were working on aim and control. Les and I agreed that until I was able to produce adequate Kara on my own, without him, he would be my training partner.

"Can you feel it under your skin?" He asked as I tried to concentrate on the Kara, I could feel rippling under my epidermis towards my palms. I could sense it moving along my arms and legs.

"Yes, it feels tight."

"That is because it is ready to be released. Focus, breathe, and let go." He steadied himself as I felt the Kara seeping from my hands. The teal mist floated toward his torso and slowly evaporated as it contacted the Philex suit he wore.

"How do I get it to really shoot out? Does it ever form into more of a stream then a mist?"

I had been growing more and more frustrated with my feeble Kara.

"Yes, the Kara will become stronger the more you practice control and force. You will need to concentrate all the Kara to your palms and release all of it simultaneously, but remember that Kara is energy and the more powerful your stream the quicker your supplies will dwindle. Now try again, I can see the Kara seeping out along your stomach and feet."

Adeline and I had been allowed to make the switch from our training suites into our proper Kara warrior uniforms; we were now located on opposite sides of the arena from each other.

I could see Judas and Runn to one side of me, working on the same tactics. Judas had the opposite problem I did. He could not stop his Kara from releasing all at once, but he was also not able to focus in on one location, and so usually expressed all of it across his body in one quick burst. He stopped to drink Yurrlu three times so far.

Ming was practicing her production and release with Tikk on the other side of Judas. Alva and Ming had more trouble with buildup than anything. Alva, partnered with Innc, was struggling a few steps behind Ming and Tikk. Both women could usually concentrate on a specific area for release rather easily, but there was never much Kara produced. I could see Alva growing disgruntled, which resulted in a puff of Kara escaping along her arms. She would then realize that her emotional reaction was working in her favor and the process would start again. Tikk kept running at Ming or jostling her to get her excited enough to produce a decent amount of Kara.

Further down the line, I could make out Lyttl, a massive warrior who stood a foot above all his fellow Par with a bright disposition to match his bright yellow skin, working with Bo who was taking a break and drinking a bright orange Yurrlu. Lyttl towered over Bo and was looking down at his new training partner with compassion.

Shurr was working with Adeline, who was coming along extremely well. Better than me, since she was able to conjure a good Kara stream without needing to be agitated by an outside source. Shurr was giving her instructions but I was too far away to hear.

The Par were fantastic coaches. They were patient and calm during our blunders and always up for trying new tactics to get us where we needed to be. I watched as Bryyl brought his trainee, Odelia, a jug of orange Yurrlu as I heard Les clearing his throat.

"Are you hungry?" I turned my face back to see Les had moved towards me. "You should always maintain a high level of reserves."

"I'm fine." I said and returned my gaze to the parings of Par and human that surrounded us. "I'm looking at everyone's colors." Each human had a color unique to their Kara. Ming was a light grey-blue and Judas was electric white. Adeline had a dark purple Kara that resembled Les' complexion. My eyes were drawn in her direction every time she emitted.

Kang's dark green Kara caught my eye as he thrust it full force at Yurrh, a bright red Par male who was still new to me. The room was a rush of color and motion and I was intoxicated by my new job.

"Elinor, since you do not seem interested in continuing your Kara training, I believe it is a good time for a run around the arena."

My head jerked back to see Les standing with his arms crossed and a smug grin etched across his face. I wanted to splatter Kara all over his obnoxious expression, but, strangely, no Kara formed and so I sneered at him as I jogged past.

***

The day of the banquet arrived like any other day, and I started it by running alongside Tikk as he talked strategy. "The worst thing you can do is get caught standing still on the battlefield. Remember, the Vokkna are in their environment; there is no escaping them." Tikk said as he and I led the group in circles around the immense arena.

"But if they catch me can't I just release my Kara?" I gasped. "Why isn't the strategy to surrounded them and then just release everything?"

"That is a strategy we use at times, but you could expend all of your Kara and find yourself stranded on the battle field with no stores and twenty more Vokkna moving in. They reproduce like microorganisms. This is where maintaining strong cardio, and control of your Kara come into play."

Tikk turned to face the others running behind us.

"What if you just killed the entire enemy army in one huge burst? Could that physically happen, or I suppose it would be too risky; friendly fire and all?"

Tikk continued to run backwards as he answered me. "The strongest Kara attack ever formed was created by Les."

He paused and gave me a sidelong glance as he allowed his information to sink in. "He killed over three hundred Vokkna in one release and was able to target them on the battlefield so that no Par lives were lost. If you have hopes in that strategical direction, I recommend you speak to your training partner about it."

We passed Les as he and two other Par unloaded a cargo ship. Les had taken on a much more managerial role during training. He spent most of his time going over charts and sending and receiving intelligence briefings from Hurran. We agreed it would be best if he didn't come near me unless we were working on Kara control. He was the only thing that could get me to build up my stores. I could go an entire day without an episode and then one glance from Les and my whole body would erupt.

By that evening I was more impatient than ever with my inability to form Kara without Les being near me. Shurr was attempting to calm my frustrations to no avail as he said, "The Kara is linked to your emotional state, so it is no surprise that he is a trigger for your build up."

We were doing a quick control training session before we had to get ready to leave for the banquet. Shurr, one of our many commanding officers, had formed us into groups and he, Runn, and Innc were instructing us in release technics.

"Be happy that your Kara is strong. Ming and the others are having difficulty building up any kind of supply. You are a very emotional creature."

I raised my head so he could see the bitchy look I was giving him. We stood in the corner of the training arena. Runn, Shurr, and Innc were in full Philex garb while the rest, except Judas and Bo, who refused to wear the shorts, lined the walls in traditional Philex fighting gear.

Judas and Ming flanked me. Adeline, Talbot, Alva, and Bo were to the right of Ming and Kang, Luke, Ansely, and Odelia stood to the left of Judas. Ansely, Adeline, and I were the only ones that could push out a healthy stream with some semblance of control, but I was limited to the times when Les was actually around, so I was just as worthless as the majority of them for the moment.

"I apologize for the interruption." Urral had just entered the room and was waving his hands above his head.

"Les has arrived with your clothing for the banquet and it is time for us to prepare for departure. Please clean yourselves and you will find your new garments in your sleeping chambers."

He turned on his heel and exited but then quickly jogged back in.

"Ming, I will see you in the cargo area once we are ready, and we will all leave together."

Realizing he had forgotten to announce this detail to the rest of us he raised his voice and repeated himself.

"New clothes, hell yeah!" Ming exclaimed as she linked her arm in mine and angled us toward the exit. "I'm dying to see what they wear other than black."

I couldn't help but be curious myself. We had not ventured far outside the arena since arriving. I had only seen the buildings of Sharron from far away and was eager to meet more Par and learn more about our new world.

By this time everyone had properly spread out and claimed their own room around the arena. I was now located on the fourth floor. Ming, Judas, Bo and Alva shared my floor but we each had our own room and facilities. I had grown to enjoy their closeness in proximity more than I thought possible.

"I for one am excited to see what a Par female looks like" Bo followed Ming and me up the stairs and I could hear Judas agreeing with him from a few steps down.

"Actually, I am curious as to what a girl version of Les looks like." I shrugged, as I turned towards my private bath, but was stopped short when Ming didn't let go of my arm.

"Hey, things are ok with you two, right?" She searched my face for something; I didn't know what answer she was looking for. "It's just that you've been spending a good amount of alone time with him for your Kara stuff, and despite the fact that it's always negative stuff, you seem to constantly be talking about him."

Both our eyes slanted, and both our hands went to our hips.

"If you're asking if I have moved passed him raping me then the answer is yes, it's over."

I fluttered my hand in the most nonchalant way I could. I had used the word so much that it had become an insignificant part of my vocabulary at this point.

"It only comes up every other time I see him now." I smiled at her shocked look. "I'm joking… it still comes up every time."

I laughed at this. I couldn't help myself. I was the girl that had made jokes about how my father would have disapproved of the low-quality knife they had used to behead him. The Kara was my new favorite emotional crutch, and I saw little reason to talk about something when I could transfer that anger into energy during battle.

"I'm serious Ming," I swung my hand onto her shoulder and said, "I'm ok."

"El," She mimicked my motion with her hand, so we stood facing each other, "I wasn't really worried about that."

A sly smile crept across her face and she whispered, "I just think you should know that you are starting to sound like an infatuated school girl in regard to Les, and I'm pretty sure I'm not the only one who has noticed."

She began to giggle and rested her forehead on mine. I leaned my head back and lightly shoved her nose with my own.

"You're insane." I broke our strange embrace and turned toward my facility room. "He infuriates me!" I had the sudden drive to justify myself. "I mean, I need him right now, and maybe that's why I keep thinking about him."

I paced the floor in front of the facility room and Ming watched me talk to myself in awe. "It's because my Kara depends on him is all, and as soon as I can build up stores without having to think about how much I hate him I can… I can… I don't know, kill him I guess."

I stopped and finally caught Ming's eyes in hope of

gaining her nod of approval, but I was met with the same sly smile she had begun our conversation with.

"You're seriously hung up on this guy. That's a new level of fucked up, El, think about it."

The smile shifted to a scowl as she spun and left me standing in my exasperated silence. "Stop arguing with yourself and get ready." She called over her shoulder before entering her own cleaning facility. "You can't do anything right now, so be a good female and try to look pretty."

The last thing I heard was her laughter before I stormed into my cleaning facility, stripped, and entered the beaming orange light that indicated the level of filth registered on my body. I began to tremble with anger, but I wasn't really angry. I wanted something. Needed it. Then the thought that I hadn't smelled Les in over two days came to mind, and I calmed myself with the reminder that I would be seeing him very soon. This of course only succeeded in causing me to worry about my ability to control myself when around him. Had they already thought of that and chosen an outfit that covered me properly? The light that engulfed me began to wane, which indicated that I was clean, and so I bolted toward my room to examine the clothes Urral had laid out for me.

I found a long black piece of Philex laying on my bed, and had zero idea what to do with it until Urral's disembodied voice spoke up, "Hello, this is a recording so please do not attempt to communicate. We have decided to give all of you freedom in your clothing choices. This Philex is designed to take whatever shape its owner wishes it to take. You will find a tablet inside the box beneath the Philex material. This tablet controls the material. Scroll through the clothing options or create your own version using your finger as a drawing utensil. The Philex will take any form you choose and will contour to your body once the choice is made. If you wish to change your mind, simply make a different choice on the tablet and the Philex will shift to conform. Enjoy and please be in the cargo bay by fraction 16."

I found the tablet and began to scroll through the *Female Style Options* section, but was not finding anything that struck my fancy. Most of the suggestions were minuscule. Obviously, females were not expected to be modest on Qualittia, but, then, Par females never had Kara ready to pulsate out of their pores at any moment. I slid over to check out the male's options and was much more interested in what I saw. Most of the options were full body suits similar to our training suits. I went with a deep cut body suit that covered most of my skin just in case my emotions got the best of my training, but the deep slit between my breasts gave everyone a little peek at my newly acquired abs, which I believed simply needed to be seen. There are no mirrors anywhere and so I assumed I looked as awkward as I felt and made my way to the cargo bay.

I ran into Judas and Bo as I made my way to the stairs. They both wore the basic body suit style, but Judas' was sleeveless, and Bo was working a V not quite as deep as mine.

"Looking good gentlemen." I looped my arms with theirs and had them flank me as we walked down to the bottom floor where the ship was located.

"The male and female styles don't differ too much." Bo said as he checked out my outfit.

"I actually choose this from the male section. I couldn't find anything I would be comfortable with in the women's section. The chicks on this planet all dress as if they don't have a toxin about to excrete from their skin at any moment, and I for one do not want to accidentally kill a planetary leader."

"You're not the only one in danger of disintegrating someone." Judas adjusted himself as we descended the last set of stairs. "I'm starving, but I don't want to fuel the Kara. Do you see Ansley around yet?" He craned his neck in search of his date. Bo chose to go solo and "check out the Par talent," as he put it.

"She's probably still up there trying to do something with her hair. All the girls are very jealous of Elinor and Ming's self-made hair brushes." Bo laughed as he patted my well-combed main. I had recently cut a couple segments off with a large cooking knife.

"Hey, we put in the time making those things out of random parts in the medical bay." I swung my auburn locks away from him and ran my fingers through its well-kept strands. "If those girls need to brush their hair, they can put in the time just like we did."

After our first day of training Ming and I realized we were either going to have to cut all our hair off or find a way to put it up while we trained, and we needed a way to comb out the knots; the cleansing light leaves hair soft and clean but does nothing for the tangles. It is hard for Par to understand the frustration of tangles since they have never had unconscious filaments growing from their body that they had little control over. So, after a day of constant hair yanking Ming and I had spent an afternoon fusing random parts of hardened Philex to a larger Philex rod in order to form something as brush-like as we could.

Tikk had run his calloused fingers through our tangled strands as he watched us working in the medical bay. He and Urral were more than happy to help with the cooking knife haircuts, and Urral kept the hair clippings for analysis. Neither the Par nor Harlukkna grow hair so Urral was captivated by the long, thin fibers that sprouted from our body. "It's so soft." He exclaimed as he cupped a pile of my hair in his hands and said, "I truly wish that you had not destroyed your planet. I'm sure it was an amazing world to behold."

"Elinor, this is most uncommon." Les, who had just approached Judas, Bo, and me at the bottom of the stairs, pulled me back to the present. He appeared unhappy and from one look at our identical outfits I knew what he was so peeved about. He gestured between us. Judas and Bo began to giggle.

"You are the ultimate gross couple." Bo said before he and Judas broke down into full on laughter. Les did not see the humor and quickly silenced the men with a rage filled look.

"You will have to change." He was now sending the look my way. "We cannot be in identical patterns. Why did you not choose from the female section?" Les and I were standing alone now, and I was starting to get nauseous.

"Stop being an asshole or I'm going to spew Kara all over everyone." I crossed my arms in defiance. "Why don't you go change? I don't want to wear something that gives me zero coverage." I shrugged at his perplexed look. "It's not modesty; I'm worried... I mean, I've only been around you for a minute and I'm already about to erupt." I met his eyes and his scent snuck into my olfactory glands. "Maybe I shouldn't go."

He stepped back in surprise. "No, you are the most important aspect of our plan." He paused and I could see him rethinking what he was about to say. "You are the most promising Kara warrior at the moment, and we need to be able to show the elders progress." He rubbed his hand along the back of his head, and I could see his anxiety.

I didn't care about making his life any easier, but I didn't enjoy his pain as much as I had hoped.

"I get it." I put my hands between us and said, "I'll go and change. It will still be a male's style, but it would be weird if we dressed the same." I turned and headed back up the stairs.

I had reached the second floor by the time I noticed Les quietly trailing me. I stopped and without turning said, "You don't need to accompany me. I can figure it out." He took the opportunity to get ahead of me, so I was forced to follow him.

"I have decided that I will change instead" He did not look at me and sped up as he spoke. "The pattern looks better on you than me, and I do not care much for these events... and the evening is for you anyway." The way he spoke made it sound like he in fact cared very much so I continued my set course.

"Oh, so now you're suddenly mister amiable?" I scoffed as I nearly sprinted up the stairs to keep up with his pace. "What are your plans for tonight? Why do I feel like you are pandering to me, so I'll behave in front of all your elders and whatnot?"

"Because that is exactly what I am doing." He reached the top of the stairs and made a beeline for his room. I had unconsciously followed him and was also unconsciously entering his room after him. He turned to face me, "They are not the wealthiest men on Qualittia because they give their money to anyone who asks. We will need to prove that you are what we claim before they will fund us. The Par cannot afford another failed attempt at war with the Vokkna, and many of these men have already earn profits from trade with the Vokkna. Tonight, must go perfectly, or we will receive no support." He grabbed the tablet that was laying on his bed and began scanning for a new pattern.

I walked so that I could see the screen and indicated a style that was comprised of long pants, but with a stylized waste made of three bands that worked their way up his torso. I pointed and said, "Just go for that one. We already know you're big and muscly; you don't have to be shy."

He met my eyes and said, "It is not appropriate for the evening, but I appreciate your complement, even if it was not meant as one." He smiled at my narrowed eyes and selected a pattern with a deep swoop in the top half instead of a V.

"Yes, the off the shoulder look is much classier." I giggled as his Philex shifted shape as I spoke. "Can we go now? I'm sure everyone is waiting on us." I began to turn but Les caught my arm and forced me to look into his black orbs.

His scent wafted across me as he said, "Elinor," The name always sounded different on his lips. "I know things are tense between us now, and I know I have had a part in this, but I need for us to work together. If I cannot..." His grip around my arm tightened and I flinched before I could control myself. He released me and continued with his hands behind his back. "If you do not wish to be with me physically, I will accept your choice, but you must be willing to work with me to defeat our common enemy."

My arms were cold where he had released them; I rubbed them for warmth and said, "Just tell me what I need to do at this thing to get the old guys to give us the money."

17.

Les and I talked strategy during the short ride to the banquet. We loaded onto one of the Par's cargo ships and leapt to the city of Typpyton. It only took twenty minutes from loading to leap so there wasn't much time to get our plan straight before we were to meet the govenors. We finished our conversation in whispers as we exited the ship and made our way toward a massive, and of course, white, building that stood among many other large structures. As the trade and business hub of Qualittia, Typpyton is not a pretty city but very functional. Nothing was manufactured on Qualittia anymore, but anything to do with commerce was taken care of in Typpyton.

"You have me so freaked out that I might spew Kara at any moment." I was clinching my teeth at Les as Ming and Urral walked beside us.

"Do you need a moment alone? Now is the time to express Kara. Once inside the grand hall all eyes will be on you."

Les leaned in to keep our conversation as quiet as possible.

"Well, then yes, I probably should."

I stopped, causing Alva, Runn, and Bo to hesitate.

"Sorry, go ahead. I need a pit stop." I waved them past and stepped to the side of the walk way. The cargo ship had popped into a spot just outside of the building, which housed Main Communications, the most powerful company on Qualittia at the time, and of course the man we had come to impress was Grymmig, the leader of Main Communications, and the true villain of our story.

Qualittia's large sun had set and its three clustered moons could be seen clearly as I stepped behind some foliage and allowed my Kara to slowly seep from my pores.

"Ok, I'm feeling better." I said as I joined the others.

"If you feel yourself begin to lose control tell me, and I will escort you to a safe area." Les nodded at me and then placed his hand on my lower back and guided me toward the intimidating structure, which resembled all the others in the vast city, but lacked the large viewing portals commonly found in Par architecture.

"Where are all the portals?" I asked as we reached a line to the main entrance.

"Grymmig claims views lower productivity."

Les grimaced to show me he did not agree.

"Do not worry, we are going to the roof where there is a beautiful view of the sky."

We stepped forward in line as I watched Judas and Ansely nod to the red Par male reading from a tablet at the head of the line and entered some kind of free standing elevator. The small portal they entered was quickly sealed and then leapt to the top of the building.

"That thing certainly moves quickly." My eyes widen as I nudge Ming. She and Urral had waited for us while I had my Kara moment.

"Why don't you guys have that at the arena? Would sure save my ass from going up and down stairs all day." Ming said as her grip on Urral's bicep tightened.

"Those devices are only being used for this event. Grymmig doesn't want any riffraff in his building," Les replied as his hand slowly moved up and down my lower back. There was a comfort in knowing that if I did slip up and release my Kara, he would be the first one to drop dead.

"Besides, you need all the motion you can get while you are in training," Les added with a quick snarl at Ming. "These devices are for the weak and old."

Urral and Les had a private laugh at his comment while Ming and I rolled our eyes in unison. Urral and Ming had arrived at the front of the line and were now facing us as the pod door closed. The Par at the front of the line gave me a look up and down before indicating that Les and I could enter the pod once it reappeared at eye level.

"He is judging your choice in pattern," Les whispered to me as we entered.

I leaned towards the red Par and said, "Don't be jealous that I look way better in this than you ever would," before the door closed,

Les burst into laughter as the pod door opened. "I do not believe that was the cause of his disapproving look, Elinor."

"I know but fuck that guy and anyone who assumes they know what I should wear."

The roof was at least three hundred meters wide and even longer. Music that greatly resembled the sound of the wind came from somewhere while colorful Par dressed in various styles of Philex moved across the open floor area. Long tables of strange foods were laid out on the opposite side of the room from the open area. The planet's two moons seemed so big and close that I couldn't help but reach my hand toward the full, white spheres that rested above the swaying Par. I tore my eyes from alabaster satellites and turned to Les.

"This is a legitimate party." I must have been smiling because that was the expression Les gave me in return.

"I am glad you are pleased. It would probably be best to eat before meeting Grymm and the other goveners." He said as he guided me toward the buffet.

This being the first time Les had discussed his plans with me I had yet to register the name, so I said, "I'll bite. Who is Grymm?"

As we made our way around, the Par seemed to hover in the air as they danced. This was my first encounter with a Par female, and I became distracted by the fluid movement of their bodies.

"Is that…" I had stopped short, which caused Les to bump into me, and I was trying my hardest not to point at what I knew was a Par female moving flawlessly across the floor in choreographed motion to the music.

"Is that what all your females look like?"

My answer was as simple as looking around the rest of the crowd. Yes, they were all tiny and gorgeous and dancing in unison to the beat. The one I was currently referring to was aqua in color and about half my size. She looked like I did at age twelve but with none of the awkwardness.

"I know, they're fucking gorgeous and it's fucking pissing me off." I knew it was Ming behind me without turning and I knew she was referring to the Par females.

"Our females do not please you?" Les was looking between Ming and me in confusion. "They are small, but they do serve their purpose well."

I couldn't keep the look of contempt from my features.

"I am not going to understand what you are upset about unless you communicate with me." Les had removed his hand from my back and both he and Urral were backing away cautiously.

"Ok," I waved my hands across my body in an X to bring myself and Ming back to the present. "Some serious issues have just come to light, but this is not the time to discuss everything that was wrong with your statement. We need to focus on the prize, but just know we are having this discussion when we get back to the arena."

I pushed past Les and began examining the large spread of multicolored food. Les was right behind me followed by Ming and then Urral who was constantly checking around the crowd for something. Our arrival had made an impact on the Par. As more of our group made it onto the roof the more murmuring I could hear. I found a large plate and began to load it up and then I remembered that there was an important person I needed to impress. I looked to Les and asked, "So, Grymmig, Grymm, who am I supposed to be impressing?"

"Grymm and Grymmig are both short names for Grymmiganactla 5354, the Par in control of everything you see." Les was also pilling his plate high with purple, pink, green, and yellow bits of goodness. I mostly copied whatever he grabbed, I was starving by this point so didn't really care what was going to be shoveled into my gullet.

"He is the old man sitting to your left at the far end of the roof. His mate and son are on either side of him, and his business partner is sitting on the other side of his son."

I could see the man he was indicating. He was one of the few Par sitting at the long rectangular tables that lined the outer edges of the room. He did appear older than Les, but my previous conceptions of old had not prepared me for the Par's aging process. It was Grymm's black color that indicated his age; a Par's skin can no longer hold pigment once it reaches senility.

Les continued, "He is who we must impress, but not until he indicates that he wishes for us to approach him."

Les gave me a warning glance as we zigzagged our way towards the tables on the right side of the rooftop at an angle away from Grymm and his family.

"I get it, girls don't get to approach boys." I set my plate on the table a bit too heavily and sat with more haughtiness than I had intended. "So, what's with your females? Why are they so tiny?"

Urral and Ming sat beside us and I could see Bryyl assisting Alva in her food choices back where we had just been standing. Judas, Ansley, and Bo were on the dance floor attempting to imitate the female Par's fluid motions. Les shifted in his seat and glanced in Urral's direction for assistance

Urral gave Ming a nervous look then said, "Our females have always been petite, but when our species began to evolve past barbaric survival our cultures emphasis on female beauty focused on child rearing and physicality. Females were never expected to take part in combat or strenuous activity of any kind, and those that did were usually of a lower class. There are females working in the Muuntur Quadrant that are a bit larger in size, but Par females don't grow above one length." He paused but everyone else at the table had food in their mouth so Urral continued, "The Harlukkna are similar in size to your species, but the Harlukkna are a combined sex, so that is not a good comparison." Again, he paused. I could hear Les gulping awkwardly on my left but had no intention of lightening the mood.

"So, the males evolved to a larger size while the females were kept small?" Ming interjected.

"No, actually it is the opposite. As our females evolved to smaller sizes, we remained large."

"So, their ability to be self-sufficient evolved away?" Ming said as she and I both crossed our arms in defiance.

"I have never thought of it that way." Urral responded with his average monotone. "But, yes, that is accurate."

"This is why your species fascinates us so much." Tikk came out of nowhere. "I heard your conversation while I was dancing with Hyyan and had to come by and save you from yourself." Tikk pointed to another tiny female Par that was making her way from the dance floor to the buffet table. "That is the beauty of our cultures colliding. We will be able to learn from each other and change accordingly."

"Tikk, I haven't seen you all day, where have you been?" I reached across the table to take his hand in mine. "Will you show me some dance moves?"

Les grunted as I spoke.

"Yes, of course, but when are you to speak with Grymmig?" He looked at Les. "I know he is aware of your presence, and the sooner he agrees to fund us the sooner he will make his big speech and we can all get out of here." I was reminded of Les and my earlier conversation and began to search the area for Kang but could not find him.

"Tikk, did Kang come to the banquet?" I asked as I scanned the area.

"He decided to remain behind with the others. I believe I scared him a bit with my advances, but he has promised to meet with me this evening after I have returned." Tikk laughed to himself and said, "I suppose that is why I am so eager to return home."

"Hello all." Alva said as she and Bryyl arrived and started to clean their plates. Mine was already empty and I could feel my tummy craving more.

"Hey Tikk," Alva leaned across to meet his eyes and said, "I spoke with Kang earlier today and you have him all kinds of obsessed." She and Tikk giggled simultaneously and I felt like we were all children again. For a moment I was comforted in the purity of sexual attraction and its way of bubbling up in even the direst of situations.

Alva caught her breath and continued, "How did you know? I mean, he lived on that rock thirty-eight years and no one ever said anything, and the first week he's here an alien prince charming comes in and sweeps him off his feet." She twirled one of the dark red leaves she was eating in the air to add a bit of flare to this statement.

Tikk's gurggly laugh worked its way out of his throat and he said, "I have a way with these things, and he couldn't keep his eyes off me from day one so how could I not make a move."

"Ah, but I remember when you first mentioned him to me." Les was smiling broadly at his friend. "It was like we were back in training. He could not speak of anything else the entire day after we picked you up off that planet." Tikk reached across the table and gave Les a light jab.

"And what about this one?" Tikk indicated me with his head. "You reverted back to your warrior days." He turned from Les to me with a sadistic smile and took hold of my hand. "You turned our faithful commander into a raging beast."

"The beast part I get." I slid my hand from Tikk's grasp as a small magenta colored female, Whittmignactla 95667, approached us. She was a waif and covered in jewels. She had no black spikes like the warriors, but tiny blue and yellow gems were scattered across her arms and chest. She wore three bands of Philex across her waist and groin while her many ornaments covered her breast area.

"Hello," I said as she came to a stop beside Tikk, and even though he had taken a seat she stood just barely above his head.

The female was taken aback by my greeting and had to compose herself before giving us a small bow and informing Les that Grymm desired his presence.

Les looped his arm behind my back and said, "It is time." He must have seen the anxiety on my face because he then said, "You will do fine, and if you do not, I will be dead." He jumped out of his chair at the last word and held out his hand to me. The female had already returned to Grymmig's table, so we made our way unaccompanied.

"They don't have a full suit for you to wear?" I asked

as we got closer to Grymmig and his bored looking companions.

"Elinor, you will be successful. You have completed drills like this in practice. It will be simple, and I will do all the talking. Then we will go home and be able to focus on our real goal." He rubbed my lower back and I felt slightly better.

"I don't feel any Kara build up," I told him as we approached Grymmig.

He whispered, "I was prepared for that, and am ready to say whatever your feeble female brain needs to hear in order to properly build up Kara stores."

He smiled at my startled expression, turned to Grymm and his family and said, "Grymmig, it is a pleasure to see you as always, but I believe we can skip the formalities and get right down to the business at hand." He turned to me and I could feel the Kara boiling in the pit of my stomach. I glanced at the small female, which only caused my Kara further irritation.

"This is the female... human... you spoke of in our correspondence." The large black alien looked me over the same way he would a new toy. "She is all you described and more, but can she preform the way you promised?" He looked back at Les. The govener did not expect or want me to speak for myself. The Kara was really starting to make me sick now.

"She will out preform us all by the time her training is complete." Les beamed like a proud father and I felt my fortitude grow, but that caused the Kara to ease off, so I concentrated on how angry my new boss made me feel instead. "Elinor, please, give Grymmig a demonstration." Les stepped towards the edge of the roof away from the rest of the group and patted his Philex covered stomach. I had done this literally hundreds of times in the arena, but only about a fourth of those hit their mark.

I stood facing Les, shook the voices out of my head, lifted my hands and released all my energy. A beam of perfectly lined aqua mist shot forth from my palms and rammed into Les' abdomen. The thrust was more than he had expected; he was thrown from his position and nearly off the roof, but a laughing Grymmig stood and caught him, returning him to a balanced stance.

"Very well done my boy. I have not seen a Kara stream in many years," Grymm said, patting Les on the back.

There was much hand shaking and congratulating, but no one acknowledged me.

"You will have all the funding you need. Screw those Vokkna bastards and their boorgant. I would much rather own the land and end this foolish trade deal, and to be honest it would give me great personal pleasure to watch each and every one of those monsters die a Kara death." Grymmig nodded toward me the way he would a pet that just brought him his slippers. "I'll speak with Vyssa, Juool, and Rallun tomorrow-get this war back up." He pulled Les in close, but I could still hear them speaking.

"Tell me boy, what is the plan of attack? The Peace

Summit I assume."

Les pulled away from Grymmig's hold and returned his hand to its rightful place on my lower back. "All that is yet to be determined. You will be the first to know as soon as we have a definitive plan, but for now I believe we will call it an early night. We have much training to do." Les pushed me towards the pods, but Grymmig wanted more now that he knew we could deliver.

"We must do an image for the public. You know how the public loves to be informed, and I believe a new species on planet is a worthy topic; a bother but also a necessity." In his day Grymmig was master of the media. The masses worshiped the image he had created for himself.

"Yes, of course, a couple quick ones, but then we must get back. The humans must continue their training, and sleep is a dire requirement." I was attempting to smile at the bright red girl, the one I would soon refer to as Whitt, who sat a couple paces from where I stood but she would not lift her gaze from her empty plate.

"Come Elinor," Les whispered in my ear. "We will get some prints of you, Judas, and Bo for the public."

I scowled at him but did not argue. The quicker I did what they said the quicker I could get home.

"Here," Grymmig said, as he adjusted us into a pleasing formation. "It will be simple. Just stand still."

"What, you don't want us to smile," I said, as I examined their somber expressions.

"Of course not, who smiles in prints?" Grymmig scoffed at the ridiculousness of my statement and I could not keep a straight face after that. Numerous Par surrounded us and lifted small tablets into the air and began taking the first prints of humans on Qualittia. Most of the prints cut out Bo and Judas, which angered them beyond the appropriate level. The idea of a female Kara warrior was new and exciting to the Par, and I was Grymmig's key to winning support for the most recent installation of the Vokkna war.

"And let's do a video of the female expelling her Kara. Give the public a real show."

Grymmig was in his element now, and if his comments hadn't caused me to build up Kara stores, I would have refused his lame attempt at recreating the moment. "Everyone back away, but be sure to get me in the frame," Grymmig said.

The crowd did as it was told and I gave Les a pleading look.

"Just do as he says. You'll be fine." He returned to the edge of the wall and Grymmig moved a bit too close to me.

"I think you should back off; I'm not technically an expert yet." I half sneered half smiled at the media hound, but he merely leaned in closer.

"I have all the confidence in you. I find your species incredibly fascinating, and I now understand why Les was so quick to purchase you."

His smile broadened and he addressed the press. "This is Elinor. She is the first female and the first human to ever receive the Kara, and she is showing great promise. She is a part of our new Kara warrior regiment. Watch carefully, you are about to see something that has not occurred in over twenty rotations." His smile returned to me and he stepped back but was still close enough to remain in the picture.

Grymmig was better at generating my Kara than Les. I focused my gaze on Les and the Kara settled down. I shut my eyes tightly and reminded myself of the hate I felt towards the male standing before me.

"The devices are ready whenever you are my dear." Grymmig said, his voice flooding me with Kara.

I tuned to Grymmig and said, "You're great motivation," then raised my left arm, aimed towards Les' beautiful body, and pushed a florescent stream of turquoise mist in a perfect line towards his abdomen. I quickly remembered how the stream had caused him to nearly fall before, and that there was no one close enough to keep him from falling this time. Before I could call out for someone to catch him my Kara transitioned from a stream pressing against Les' stomach to a dark green cloud behind him, projecting him toward me. I lowered my hand. A gasp came from the crowd. My eyes were locked on Les' as he stood mouth agape staring at me and holding my hips.

"You had total control Elinor. You made the Kara hold me, lift m." He leaned in closer and said, "It was your desire for my safety that motivated you."

I had forgotten about the horde of picture takers until Grymmig forced his way between us and angled us towards the dozen of waving devices.

"Les, you didn't tell me the girl was a prodigy. This was already top news but now," Grymmig's arm encircled each of our necks and began to shake both Les and me vigorously as he continued, "Now we are going to be flooded with donations to the cause. We can get this whole thing paid for by the public." The grin on Grymmig's face was causing my Kara to creep up again so I shot Les an irritated look and thrust my head in the direction of the exit pods.

Les pulled himself free from Grmmig's grasp and said, "We really must be going now. Elinor is going to be tired after such exercion, and we obviously have much to do within a small time frame." Les slightly bowed and Grymmig did the same, then Les looked to Tikk and said, "Let's get out of here."

"Finally," Tikk said as he began to push everyone toward the pods. "Come on, if you're currently calling the arena your home makes your way to the pods."

"Until we see each other again, Elinor." Grymmig watched us leave.

"You will be in my thoughts. Les," It was as if he had just seen him, "do keep me informed of your progress, and any needs you might have." His eyes never left me. "We don't want our little warrior left wanting do we?"

"Leave Elinor's needs to me." Les' hand circled around my waist.

We said nothing else until we were on a pod heading down. As we stood close, in the confined space, my nose was once again filled with Les' scent and I could not help myself but lean into his chest to get a better whiff.

"Elinor, are you smelling me?'

I jolted upward but the small pod hindered my backward motion. I pulled back as far as the tight space would allow and said, "Well, yes, you smell really good actually."

The pod popped into place and we stepped onto the pathway. I saw Ming and Urral walking ahead of us. "Hey Ming," I ran a little to catch up with her leaving Les and his scent behind. Ming and Urral stopped and turned to face me as I said, "Did you see that crazy move up there?"

"El, that was awesome!" She grabbed my shoulders and shook them as an abandoned looking Les joined us. "Why didn't you guys tell us the Kara could do stuff like that?"

"I did not even consider it a possibility for another few lunations of training, but it appears that Elinor does not like to follow commonality or reason." Les brushed my back with his hand as I walked ahead of him. He did not touch me again the entire journey, and his inaction bothered me more than I expected.

18.

We were back in Sharronn within half a fraction. Everyone was abuzz with the night's events. Bo and Alva cornered me in the hallway and began questioning me about the Kara manipulation. I was thankful for the distraction from Les, even though I could not give them a straight answer about how I controlled my Kara the way I had. As we walked towards our separate rooms Les brushed past me and his scent caused a shiver up my spine. I bristled as he shifted away and gave me a cautious look.

He said, "I will see you in the morning Elinor. Sleep well," as he jumped up the stairs two at a time. He couldn't wait to get away from me. I was now the predator.

My thoughts of the hunt were interrupted by Tikk who said, "Elinor, are you hungry after your Kara presentation? I am meeting Kang in the dining hall for a late snack and would be happy for the added company."

I gave Tikk a questioning glance and said, "You want me to chaperone you and Kang? Are you a bit nervous?" I slid my arm through his and let him lead me up the stairs. I was hungry, and I didn't mind being used as a tension easing tool for Tikk if he needed it.

"It is not that." Tikk avoided my eyes as we marched up the stairs behind Judas and Ansely, who were too wrapped up in each other to pay us any mind. "It is just the first time we will really be alone together, and I can tell I make him nervous, and I do not want him to feel like I am pushing him in any way."

"Well, that's a unique way for males of your species to think." I envisioned Les in his chambers, but instead of the nauseous Kara feeling I was met with an ache in my loins. My emotions were shifting without my permission and I was starting to get confused.

"Do not judge Les' actions too harshly." He patted my arm as we reached the top floor and continued towards the dining hall. "He was raised in a world where he had final say in everything. He was top of his squadron in training and made commander as soon as he entered the Kara warrior fleet. Not to mention that males in our culture are taught from birth that females are for pleasure and breeding… and little else."

Kang was already there when we arrived, and I was met with an unhappy look. Tikk quickly said, "Elinor needs a snack before bed." Kang's features loosened as Tikk continued. "She expelled quite a bit of energy tonight. This looks delicious. You are going to take Mei's job if she does not watch out." Tikk was referring to the bounty Kang had been preparing when we arrived.

"Mei helped me." Kang flashed red at the admittance.

"I don't want to eat all your lovely prepared food. Is there any left over Yurrlu in the fridge?"

I slid open the large fridge and found a jug of bright purple Yurrlu waiting for me. Mei, who officially took over as arean chef by this time, usually made extra in case one of us needed an in between meal chug. I grabbed the container and said, "This is perfect." I went to the cabinet nearest the exit where I knew the smaller jars were kept and poured myself a helping from the large container.

"How was the banquet?" Kang asked as I sipped my meal. "Pretty boring around here. I found an interesting hologram though. Actually, pretty funny, but I could probably have used you for some cultural references." Kang said this to Tikk and the two of them smiled; which gave me the intense urge to leave.

"The banquet went splendidly. Elinor impressed everyone with skills I do not believe she even knew she had." Tikk smiled at me.

"You're right. I don't know if I'll be able to duplicate it anytime soon, but I'm sure as hell going to try." I gulped down the last of my Yurrlu and made for the exit. "You boys enjoy the rest of your evening."

"Elinor," Tikk stepped towards me and lowered his head, "you must understand how much you have altered Les in the short amount of time you have known him. He does everything with you in mind." He stroked my shoulder. "Sleep well Elinor."

I nodded and left the room, but I was not able to make myself go down the stairs. I decided to let my feet go where they chose, and soon found myself standing in Les' chamber. He was near the portal staring at a hologram that hovered above his face. I had made it half way into the room before either of us became aware of it. He turned to find me and we both stood silently for many moments before he started to say, "Elinor, I..."

"No," I raised my hands with my palms facing him. I locked onto his gaze and stated, "I don't want you to speak again tonight." He did as he was told.

I didn't think. I removed my Philex suit. Les immediately followed my lead and made several steps in my direction as he did. His hand slid over his head and down his neck in his usual contemplative way. I stepped forward, placed both palms on his chest, and thrust him towards the mattress as I quickly retreated to the far corner; a turquoise mist was already sprouting from my tingling epidermis. The release was sensational. I could kill him. Wipe him away. He would not be here anymore, but how would I ever forgive myself?

I lunged on top of him. Held his torso with my thighs and pushed his chest further into the cushion as my hands slid from his breast to the curve below his neck. I could feel his pulse underneath me.

Mine. Les is mine.

His breath came in sharp bursts, big hands gripped my thighs and torso licentiously, but he did not emit a sound. I rode him. Using his thick neck as leverage. Satisfaction washed over my body and our smells began to mingle. My Kara pulsated against my skin, but I maintained control. I did not need Kara release to gain pleasure with Les.

Suddenly, everything flexed and collapsed. A sigh parted Les' lips and I rolled away, but his grip on my hips remained firm, hindering my immediate escape. The pain was replaced by felicity. I forgot about Les and was drifting to sleep when I was roused by his body pressing against my own. I used my arm to put space between our gasping forms.

A smile cracked his hard features as he stretched to maintain his hold on me. "You are finished with me now?”

I couldn't help but laugh at my own need for distance. "That was out of body. It was me but... I don't know, but the pain is gone. Now I can sleep."

Les shot up to his elbow. "You were in pain? Separate from the nausea caused by the Kara?”

"It was freaky. Like nothing I had ever experienced before. I couldn't stop thinking of you."

I stood and attempted to discern which Philex suit was mine. "It's gone now. Thanks, I guess." I turned to share my convivial mood with him but was met with distress.

“You need to have Urral examine you again.”

He stood and grabbed the Philex in my left hand.

“The scent, the desire for physical connection…” He began to get dressed and I followed his lead while listening to his explanation. “It is common for the females of our species to be overly sexual with their mates when they are with child. It is called a hormone surge."

“What?” Was all I could say as I suddenly sensed his spawn growing inside of me, and I wanted to claw it out.

I turned on my heel and left the room. I had completely forgotten I was naked. "Let's just go now." Les joined me in the hallway and steered me into the facilities by my forearm. I yanked myself free and moved toward the orange haze that had beamed into life when we entered.

"Touching is over. Best keep a safety gap for the rest of the night." He did not join me in the hazy light

19.

I was sitting on an exam table in the medical room as Urral hovered over me with his ever-present tablet fixed securely in front of his face. I desperately needed him to tell me I was in fact not pregnant and could go to my room and crawl into bed.

"If I am pregnant what does that mean?" I said as I tried to catch their attention, but they refused to take their gazes from the screen in front of my torso.

"What are my options?"

"Options?" Urral finally pulled his eyes away from his tablet to look at my face. "You are pregnant Elinor. This is a fantastically exciting occurrence."

Les stood up straight and I noticed the broad smile stretched across his face.

He rubbed the back of his head with the palm of his hand and met my blue eyes with his lifeless black ones.

"This was not expected, but I am pleased."

I now had their total attention. They were waiting for me to say something, but I could not muster anything positive.

"Elinor, do not be scared." Urral placed the tablet on the table behind him and took my hand.

"This is going to be a first for all of us, and even though it is exciting I understand that you must have worries. I want you to feel free to ask me anything."

He patted my hand awkwardly and picked the tablet back up. “Your DNA is melding with Les’ in a unique way. Your egg is at the beginning stage of fertilization, but it already exhibiting aspects of both of our species maturation process.”

“You can see all of that already?” My mind was racing. I wanted nothing to do with any of it.

I was a Kara warrior and I was getting damn good at it. My future had been altered in an instant. Les and Urral were already planning out my pregnancy. Les was nodding approvingly and I was struck with the urge to hurl.

“Get away from me.” I interrupted and both men backed away from me quickly as teal Kara seeped from my pours.

I felt much better as I asked, “Can I not do this? Can I abort it? Do you have that?”

I searched their faces for a sign of understanding. Les looked thoroughly perplexed and Urral was slowly piecing together what my request meant.

"No, what you are asking goes against everything I have ever been taught. The thought that you would not want to help propagate your species confuses me." Les got the hint and they both stared at me in disgust. "Why would you not want to see what kind of life Les and you have created? You have created something completely new. Does that not excite you?"

I then became a bit more than disgusted with them,

"Because this is my body. It's a parasite growing inside of me that will eternally link me to a man I have no desire to be connected to."

I glared at Les as I finished my statement. There was no holding back now, so I continued. “I am a Kara warrior now and the best one you guys have. I came to this planet to fight, not be your experimental baby-maker.” I was in full on feminist rant mode at this point. “This is my body and you have no right telling me what I can and cannot do to it.” I pounded my chest and jumped off the table. I was naked and very primal looking, which I hoped added to my argument, but in the end did little for my cause.

Urral stepped between a silent Les and a heaving me.

"In all reality, your feelings on the matter account for little, Elinor." I pulled back at this and he continued, "Your obvious displeasure and your current status as a Kara warrior does not dispel the fact that you are Les' property. It is his choice what to do with the maturing cells growing in your womb.”

Urral nodded towards Les, whose head snapped to face me as if he expected me to spew Kara at him right then and there. Somehow, I managed to listen to the rest of Urral's little speech without decimating them both. "And I have never in all my years of being a physician heard of someone not wanting to allow a healthy fertilized egg to mature into a child." He tried to reach out to me, but I had none of it. “I believe I have the ability to do what you ask, but I will not do this for you. I have never had this request made of me.”

They had taken away my choice, but I was in no way going to let this go without a fight.

"Then you have obviously never thought to ask a female her feelings on the matter. I know that in your culture females are for breeding and little else, but in mine...." A lump had formed in my throat and I could not finish my statement. Instead I said, "I'll fight you. I'll go to Grymmig. Tell him his star warrior got knocked up and doesn't get to fight anymore." I pushed out my chin in an attempt at assertion.

"This is no longer about culture, Elinor." I could see the pity in their eyes, but I could not feel it. "I am not thinking about your feelings or the future life of the zygote forming in your uterus. The emotional state of an individual is of no significance to any of our governing bodies. They care only for the advancement of their motives, and this pregnancy will fall neatly under that category. The cells will be allowed to form into life and then be born. You have no say in the matter."

"Do not think this is over for a second." I gave each of them one last contempt filled look and began to leave the room then turned and said, "How much longer do I get to train?"

Les laughed lightly to himself and said, "Is that what is upsetting you so?" He took a couple of steps toward me and said, "You can train right up until giving birth. In fact, your pregnancy just might elevate your training."

Les looked to Urral who stepped forward thoughtfully. I could not help my curiosity. If this was going to happen to me, I was at least going to be informed.

"That is definitely a possibility." Urral said, "Par fetuses strengthen their mothers while in utero. They of course gain nutrients from the mother, but they also energize them and have even been known to return nourishment to their mothers when they are in need."

"What do you mean return nourishment?" I asked.

"Well," Urral stepped forward again and stroked his chin contemplatively. He was getting excited. "If a Par female with child was to be physically hurt the fetus would transfer energy and nutrients back to the mother in order to heal her quicker and ensure her survival. The fetus knows its life depends solely on its mother, and so it will give energy back in order to maintain both lives. This, of course, causes the maturation of the fetus to take longer than average, but it is a necessary side effect of saving both mother and child."

"That's actually pretty amazing." I said and Urral jumped as if he had forgotten Les and I were in the room.

"How long is a normal pregnancy?"

"About one rotation, but as I said before, there can be complications," Urral said as Les shifted uncomfortably. "I am sure there will be no problem and the child will be born… Oh" Urral looked between the two of us as if deciding which would be the worse outcome. "There is no doubt that Elinor will be pregnant during our attack on the Peace Summit." Urral flinched as Les paced toward the portal in aggravation.

I was unable to move. This was the entire point of my training. Why was I here if I couldn't even take part in battle? I sighed deeply and took hold of Urral's shoulders. "So, what if I am pregnant?" I looked after Les as he continued to pace. "You just said that I could train my entire pregnancy. If I can't fight alongside my brother and fellow warriors what the fuck am I even doing here?" I pushed Urral away and continued to argue my case to Les. "And Urral just said that the fetus will keep me alive. It might even help me in the battle. Maybe we should just forcefully impregnate all the female warriors, so we have an edge." I raised my eyebrows at Les, but he did not seem humored.

"I understand that the fact that we have created something together means very little to you, but it means a great deal to me and I will not willingly put you and our developing child in danger," Les said.

My eyes widened to twice their size as Les continued, "Urral is right about the fetus fueling the mother, but that can go to the extreme. The Vokkna will be aware of your condition and use it against you."

"Also, there is the danger that the fetus will give all its nutrients to it's mother if need be." Urral took up the explanation. "The fetus will sacrifice itself for the sake of the mother because it knows that, as the life giver, it is the mother's life that is most important. You will survive, which is what is truly important, but you could possibly eliminate the blastocyst growing inside of you if you choose to fight."

I was enraged, but also incredibly tired. "We are in no

way done talking about this, but for now I am exhausted." I glared at them both and said as I turned to leave, "Don't follow me."

They didn't.

ALVA

20.

The siren went off at the same obnoxious time the next day and I made my way back to the main arena to begin training. The a repeat of the routine we'd be following for the past lunations. I did not feel different, but I knew that everything had changed.

I approached Shurr as he shook himself out in preparation for our cardio and said, "Could we run in the city today, or at least get away from the arena? It would be nice to get a change of scenery." I was tired of running in circles, and I wanted to see the planet I was expected to save.

"I suppose we could start going off the usual trail. We will be upping the length of our morning run and we will be incorporating some strength routines into the cardio beginning today as well."

Shurr looked around at the growing number of disgruntled faces. I was aching to get moving. I couldn't wait to break away from the pack and get lost in my thoughts for a while. I always enjoyed cardio and running was the perfect opportunity for alone time.

"I guess we don't get a day of rest after our big showing last night." Judas nudged in close to me and I rolled my eyes.

"What did you do exactly?"

"Don't pretend you didn't see me on the dance floor showing all those Parvians how to shake it." He grinned as Shurr shot him a contemptuous look.

"Your trainers have been briefed on your individual strength routines so just stick with them and you will be fine," Shurr informed us.

Les did not usually join us on our morning run. He was always busy managing plans that he told me very little about. I began to ask Shurr if I should run with him and Adeline, but then caught sight of Les exiting the main cargo bay. He asked, "Are you ready?"

"Yes, think you can keep up," I hopped from foot to foot. The Kara pushed itself through the pours on the souls of my feet every time I took a step. All Kara warriors officially walk on air.

"Shurr has informed me of your endurance. I am excited to see your skills." Les mimicked my hopping movements.

"I want to run through the city," I said defiantly.

"That will be fine. The Par are fully aware of your presence and purpose, so there is no harm. Please lead the way," Les said pleasantly.

"Maybe you ought to lead." I slide my hands over my hair and formed it into a tight bun on top of my head; securing it with a small Philex band. As I stood on tiny clouds of Kara I looked up at Les and said, "Show me the city. Take me to all the prettiest places." He beamed down at me.

"A tour of your new home; long overdue." And he was off with me hurrying to fall along beside him. The Par do not believe in chit chat while training, and I was thankful for the policy. I have never been fond of idle chatter, and if you can blabber you can push yourself harder. So, Les and I had no need to communicate for the first part of our exersize and I began to enjoy his company, and the scent that came with it.

We stopped about halfway into the run; we had come to a large emerald lake. This was the first body of water I had seen since landing on Qualittia and I was mesmerized by the pure aqua color. The sky was a dry auburn and cloudless; small tufts of green brush littered the black, desert landscape, but no animals scurried across the scenery. I turned to face the city that stretched away along the horizon behind us. The white buildings stuck out from the black ground like crooked teeth.

"There is no real pollution on this planet and yet there is such advanced technology and infrastructure. How do you manage it?" I said as I caught my breath.

Les walked towards the water and began to scoop some into his mouth. In between gulps he said, "We no longer manufacture goods on Qualittia, and many of our structures are built off planet and shipped prefabricated. All our Philex materials are gorwn and harvested on Tralccore and shipped."

I joined him and we sat along the shore once we had our fill of translucent water. "Qualittia is solely a residential and business planet now. Talccore is agriculture and production. There are some factories in the Muuntur Quadrant where Philex is formulated into its many forms, but they will eventually be eliminated." I laid back and contemplated my newfound knowledge.

"So, you've just moved the pollution to a different planet?" Les leaned back on his elbow so he could look into my disapproving eyes.

"That is a way to say it. I prefer to say we outsourced our air and waste problem." He smiled at his joke.

"Oh my God, you amaze me." I could not help but laugh.

"Who is God, and why is he worthy of your declarations?" There was obviously no word in his language for the entity I was addressing.

"God isn't a person... God is an idea... a belief that humans used to have. Do you have religion? Like..." I stared off into the vast sapphire sky for a moment, "Where did life come from?"

"A belief? Life is not about belief. It does not matter what you believe, life is factual, and we are here because life here evolved into us. We are the dominant species, and on different planets different life forms have evolved to be the dominant species. That is all. Now the struggle for universal dominance has begun." His face contorted into a confused sneer. "What is religion?"

I struggled to explain the concept of theology, which I myself had never fully comprehended. "From what I have read, religion is a belief system. Usually based on the creation of life, and is usually a dictation of morals and things like that. Humans created many religions. Islam, Judaism, Paganism, Christianity, all equally absurd and harmful in their own way. Millions of humans died for various religious reasons throughout our history. None legitimate."

I spoke quickly as I remembered the history slides my father used to show me as a child.

"This all happened over a thousand years before I was even born. Most people stopped believing in a god before Kepler was colonized, but it's an idiom that stuck. Something you say when you're amazed or upset." I let my gaze linger on the skyline. "All completely pointless now isn't it?" I laughed to myself and continued to avoid his eyes.

Les remained silent for far longer than I had anticipated, and I was forced to look in his direction to ensure he was still lying next to me.

"The more I learn about you the more I am intrigued. Please tell me about humans. They seem truly horrible at life. How you survived this long I will never know." He sat up quickly and continued. "But I am pleased that humans were able to evolve enough to reach space." I didn't know how to react. I was insulted slightly, but unsure of how to argue for a culture I did not truly connect with.

So instead I said, "I want to run more. We aren't anywhere near done and I'm already getting hungry." I stood.

"If you are hungry you should eat. There is a place we can acquire sustenance near here. Follow me."

"No, Shurr said we had to complete our lengths and strengths first." Les stood beside me.

"Shurr is not aware of your condition. The cells forming within you need constant sustenance." His hands moved towards my torso and I became self-conscious.

"No, I will not be treated differently just because you put this inside of me. I have very little choices left and this is something under my control. We will complete my training and then I will eat with the rest of the squad." He did not argue, and I motioned with my arm for him to lead on.

Later we were at the training arena and I was faint from hunger. It literally felt like my insides were eating at me, and with my limited knowledge of Par pregnancy I thought that could have very likely been what was happening. I stopped sprinting just short of the entrance and entered the arena. Les followed close behind me. He had pushed me hard and my legs shook. I turned up the stairs and did high knees to the sixth floor; I might as well keep up the momentum. Les had promised to make me Juakwann beast as soon as we got back; a cleanse could wait.

Les was true to his word and within a fraction there was a large slab of purple meat laid in front of me. I had cut some shushu to eat while I waited. Les had not had time to eat any veggitation before it all ended up in my stomach.

"I feel like I am cheating on everyone." I said as I shoved a hand full of juicy meat into my mouth.

"Your condition changes everything. You cannot feed yourself and fuel the growing cells in your body with Yurrlu alone." Alva and Ming entered the kitchen with Tikk and Innc close behind. They all stopped short. Ming and Alva's eyes locked onto my hand that clasped a large chunk of Juwakkwan beast.

Ming's eyes narrowed and she asked, "Are we all getting a treat or are Les and El being a bit naughty?" She was far too pleased with herself to be angry with me.

I breathed deeply to give myself time, but it was pointless to keep anything from them. "I'm pregnant." I looked to Les during the silence that followed my revelation. "We just found out yesterday, and I'm just going to need a bit more sustenance than everyone else until this thing is out of me." I shoved the meat into my mouth so I would not be required to speak anymore.

"Holy shit, El!" Ming reached for my flat tummy and I angled myself away from her groping hands. "You literally have an alien life form growing inside of you." She crossed her arms and met my narrowed eyes. "Alright, Let's can talk about it more later." Alva took Ming's cue and did not press the topic further.

"We should really hurry to the arena." Tikk opened the large cooler and pulled out two massive jugs of Yurrlu. "The rest will be arriving soon and in need of nutrients." I grabbed a couple more slices of meat and followed them down.

21.

Strategy meetings lasted too long for my taste, but the Par had gone many years without a real war to plan for and I could tell they derived great pleasure in discussing tactics and analyzing each other's plans for our first attack.

"Stealth is our greatest ally," Les said, but he was far more interested in reminding us of his superior knowledge than in giving legitimate advice. Most of his input consisted of rejecting his comrades' suggestions but never giving any of his own.

"The longer the Vokkna remain unaware of the attack the better for us," He added.

My inability to take part in the attack had already been decided and so I had spent the past lunation zoning out during our strategic discussions.

My silence was not noticed. Les and Shurr controlled the conversation with random injections by a Par trainer every few moments. Like myself, the rest of the humans were primarily quiet during these meetings. We focused our attention on our new, transparent devices that had been programed with holographic representations of the Vokkna, the creatures we were expected to kill in about eight lunations. We were all having a difficult time comprehending the sand tornados that are the Vokkna. They did not look like living things, but they also did not look like anything I had come into contact with before so I believed Shurr when he said they were full-fledged life forms that could kill us by engulfing us in a whirlwind of matter.

"The Harlukkna will also act to stop us, and we do not wish to harm any of them. They have never reacted with violence before, but it is best to maintain our alliance with the least amount of strain." Tikk was the biggest advocate for the Harlukkna. We had not been given many details about the dominant species of planet Haurran yet.

They are a peaceful species that had created an alliance with both the Vokkna and Par, and both species respected their peaceful intentions. It was clear that Les and other Par did not hold the Harlukkna's obsession with peace in high regard, but they never mentioned causing them any harm and always spoke of them with reverence in their voice.

One Harlukkn was admired above all the others. Oolang was a Harlukkna that had fought with Les' squadron against the Vokkna during the time before the anti-Kara had been released. Oolang had returned to Hurran and began working with the peace committee when the Kara was stripped from all the warriors. It was clear that Les was eager to have his old friend rejoin the war effort.

Shurr glanced in Les' direction. All the warriors present had fought alongside Oolang, but it was clear that Les had the closest relationship with the Harlukkna warrior.

"For now, we will maintain total secrecy, but Elinor is

correct in her suggestion. We will have to inform at least Oolang at some point before the attack. Harlukkna casualties are not permitted within this mission."

"Why do we not just inform the Hurlakkna of our intentions, or at least the one, Oolang? Do you believe they would turn against you?" Talbot had interjected his comment amid the discussion. All of us had stopped waiting our turn to speak by this point. Par did not find interruptions impolite if it was a valid thought.

Shurr tilted his head as he considered Talbot's question and said, "I do not believe it would be wise to inform the Harlukkna at this point. I do not think they would inform the Vokkna of our plans, but I do think they would attempt to thwart our attack. They are very keen for this discussion to take place. Even Oolang has grown more inclined toward peace in the past years."

"You don't think the Harlukkna will give us any trouble? I mean, they're bound to defend themselves and their home," Judas said as he sat up. The padded floor of the arena always made it difficult to remain fully alert. The second day of training Shurr had caught six of us, including myself, sleeping during his lecture and we ended up doing sprint bursts the rest of the lesson. No one fell asleep during strategy meetings after that, but Shurr did not mind us resting during the discussions as long as our eyes stayed open and our brains active.

"At the most the Harlukkna will attempt to intervene orally." Lyttle smiled as he said this, but his tone was judgmental. "Even with their beautiful weapons, I have never been met with physical confrontation by any

Harlukkna other than Oolang. He was a rare jewel in their population of weaklings, and now even he has become preoccupied with this Peace Summit." Lyttle, Runn, and Fydds chuckled to themselves but Les and Shurr remained stoic.

"Oolang does what he believes is best," The Par fell silent at Les' sharp tone. "And if we had not found the humans, we would be attending this Peace Summit with our heads hung low and with every intention of submitting to the whim of the committee. I understand the populations' hopes for this discussion. It will be the first of its kind and could bring about lasting peace, but it could also bring about death and slavery to all Par and human alike. Now that we have an option other than surrender, we must be prepared for a physical and a political battle."

"The Harlukkna are our allies and will remain as such even after war has been declared." Shurr was attempting to bring everyone back to the lecture. "Our discussion today is not about alliances, but instead focused on our need for stealth within the walls of the summit building. As I said before, the Kara detectors have been dismantled, but we will need to attack as a unit in order to wipe out as many Vokkna during the initial interaction as possible. We all need to focus on Kara isolation and release control. This is the most important skill to hone during our first attack. Once war has been declared battle will be shifted back to the open fields of Valakarri and Trallcore, and our cardio training will come into play. So, we are going to be shifting our cardio time to more Kara training. We will add weight training to our morning runs and after strategy discussion we will have four fractions of straight Kara training."

No one made a sound, but dissatisfaction permeated the air. I caught Les' stare and rolled my eyes to insure he knew the thought of spending that much one on one time with him caused me despondence.

"I know this sounds excessive, but you are all lacking the basic Kara skills to take on a foe like the Vokkna. The Vokkna who will be present at the summit are prior warriors and commanders of the Vokkna ranks and will not be destroyed without a fight."

Shurr did a scan of the room. "That is part of the reason this attack is so imperative. By taking out the top members of the Vokkna military we are sending a message of war and cutting out an important segment of their strategizing force. If we fail, the war will be over before it begins, and we will most definitely be destroyed."

"Can we at least discuss what the Peace Summit actually is all about for a moment?" Adeline asked, and I seconded her question. "Why is it so important and why do we not want to be at peace?" Shurr stared back at Adeline blankly, and then shifted his gaze to Tikk who was awkwardly avoiding eyecontact.

Tikk glanced around at the other Par but was met with darting eyes, so he spoke,

"Recently, a Vokkna captive was caught and kept alive long enough to be infected with LiquiParin."

The room was silent. This was the first time the Par had openly discussed current events with us. We had only been privy to battle knowledge and old war stories regarding the Vokkna up to this moment. The Par had told us that from the first contact with the Voknna they had been at war. No communication was ever attempted on the Vokkna's end, and all captives of war had self-destructed or been killed in the process of imprisonment.

Shurr continued, "It was the first time anyone has been able to hold a captive Vokkna alive and attempt to communicate with it. It is being held on Hurran because the Harlukkna can understand it. Both their languages are rooted in movement and nonverbal communication and with assistance from the captive they have sent a message back to Valkarie to invite the Vokkan to the peace summit."

"It sounds more like a ransom than an invitation." Judas interjected.

"Yes," Les answered, "the Vokkna have never responded to any communication attempted by the Harlukkna, but this time they responded within a turn. We should have used prisoners of war rotations ago."

"So now that you are able to communicate with this Vokkna captive what have you discovered about them and their plans for peace? Why send us in to start another war?" I asked.

"That's just it, the Vokkna savage does not desire peace." Les injected and a murmur of approval came from the rest of the Par present. "We learned nothing we didn't already know. They see us as unworthy of life."

"But this is just the beginnings of our relationship with the Vokkna. Oolang has described the change that has come over the captive in the short time it has been able to communicate with the Harlukkna, and the Vokkna have agreed to attend the summit," Tikk spoke up. "If we only took the time to learn their language, we could have a real conversation. We have an amazing opportunity here for the Par, Harlukkna, and Vokkna to all be on the same planet without the intention of destroying each."

"Wait," I was struck with what Tikk said and asked, "The Par have never even attempted to learn the Vokkna language? Even though the Harlukkna have been communicating with them for a lunation?"

"There is no point. The Harlukkna have translated the Vokkna's views on the matter and they have declared war on all species not their own. From what Oolang tells me," Les' gaze jumped from Tikk to myself, "they even fight amongst their own species. The Vokkna are a murderous species that only understand force." Les scoffed as he began to walk away from the group.

"Come Elinor, enough talk of politics. Kara training begins now."

But we were far from done talking politics.

22.

"Just because a language is different does not mean that it's inferior. That is a flaw in your thinking, not a flaw in the Vokkna's language," I said as Les and I stood in the arena far from the others, who had begun their Kara training.

"I do not wish to discuss the Vokkna or their language any further."

"Well, I don't care what you want to do, we are going to talk about this. I'm appalled that this would even be something I have to suggest. Why would you not learn the Vokkna's language and make a legitimate attempt to speak with them; to create peace instead of war?" I was breaking down. I was reminded of how insignificant and inferior humans were considered only a few lunations prior to this moment, and I could not help myself but stand up for the creatures I was being trained to kill.

"They were the first to attack. They compressed our warriors into dust before the squadron had a chance to attempt communication." Les took a step back.

"And do you not think that maybe that was because you were the first contact, they had with anything outside of their planet? I'm sure you were terrifying monsters swooping down from the sky, and then what; that was it? They get one chance at a good impression and every Vokkna is considered an enemy?" I closed the gap between us.

"The Harlukkna have informed us of the Vokkna's views towards the Par, and all living creatures not Vokkna. They believe we are the inferior ones because we do not adhere to their form of science." He paused and looked around nervously, but no one could hear us. "Actually, it is similar to your description of religion." He loosened up and I could see his mind working. "I think religion is a better word for what Oolang told me of their system of thinking. We just had no other word for it. I will have to tell him of my discovery." Les smiled at me and I gave him a slight shove.

"First, you didn't discover anything. I told you about religion, and I will be the one to explain to Oolang, or anyone else. Second, I want you to take me to Hurran. If you will not learn the Vokkna language, then I will. Even if they are unwilling to end the war at least we can say we tried. Come on, no training for tonight." I turned to leave.

"Elinor, we cannot simply leap to Hurran tonight." Les followed on my heels as I headed to the top floor.

"Yes, we can, and you know it. Take me, or I will be utterly insufferable until you do." I stopped short and Les bumped into my back. "Or perhaps I will just kill you in a puff of Kara."

His eyes rolled as he pushed past me. "We will need to enlist Tikk's help if we are to leave tonight. I will inform Oolang of our arrival so he will ensure we have a meeting with the captive. We will see how empathetic you are towards the Vokkna after you have met one. Return to the arena and finish training on your own. You will not slack just because you decided to form a weakness for your enemy."

I could barely concentrate on my training that night and rushed through our final meal to the point of nearly making myself sick.

"Maybe there's more than one Par baby in there." Alva was staring at me as I gobbled down my shushu. The rest of the crew drank Yurrlu. The fact of my pregnancy had spread without any action on my part, which suited me fine. I felt a slight nudge from my left and turned to see Judas huddled over his Yurrlu and avoiding my eyes.

"Why didn't you tell me? It's not like there haven't been opportunities."

I had not thought of his feelings and was not in the mood to explain myself at that moment, but I attempted a half smile and looped my arm around his shoulder after shoving the last bite of shushu in my mouth.

"I didn't tell anybody. Ming and Alva found out and I had zero motivation to discuss it."

He still wouldn't meet my eyes, so I set my chin on his back as he stared at the floor.

"It's far from ideal, but we have to live with it now. There's no way to get rid of it and they say that I can still train."

"For how long?" Alva spoke up.

When I turned to face her, I could see we had attracted the attention of the table. Innc and Shurr were the only Par in attendance and I wondered if Les had the rest of the crew with him discussing our trip to Hurran. It occurred to me that my fellow warriors were constantly in the dark about parts of my life, and I didn't like the thought.

"I can train all the way up until the first attack, which they have forbidden me from taking part in."

Ming set down her jar with a bang and threw up her arms. "You're the best we have. Even in six months we will need you. We need each other to succeed. I get it, you're pregnant, but this sucks huge dick."

Shurr choked at Ming's statement and we all laughed as he regained his composure.

"You will be successful." Shurr straightened himself up and cleared his throat. "As long as we focus on our training and maintain the element of surprise, we will be the victors. Elinor's condition is ill-timed, but beneficial to her training in the long run."

Again, all eyes turned to me. "Well, explain," Judas said with his hand resting on the top of my back.

"A Par fetus is different from a human one, obviously." We all smiled awkwardly.

"The fetus is able to give me strength and sustenance just as much as I am able to give the same to it. It will even go so far as to sacrifice itself in order to preserve my life. That is why they do not want me fighting in the initial attack. I will be nearly ready to give birth and if I'm hurt or in need the fetus will give its life to sustain me."

I looked around at the confused faces of my peers. "It's a more mutual relationship, if not slightly skewed in my favor."

There was a long bout of silence finally broken by Odelia asking, "Then why don't all the girls get preggers so we can have that extra energy reserve? It seems like a good fail safe to have in place. If we run out of energy stores during the attack we will have a way to stay alive." She looked to Shurr who looked at the floor uncomfortably.

"I cannot speak for every Par male, but I for one would not risk the life of my unborn offspring just to have an upper-hand in battle. The fetus' contribution does not even guarantee the life of the mother. There is a large chance that both lives would be lost, and that is not a chance I am willing to take."

Innc nodded in agreement and the table fell silent again.

"I get it." Odelia shrugged and turned from the table to leave the dining area. "I'm just looking for ways to survive." I met her eyes and nodded in an attempt at solidarity. "I'm going to bed," she said as she left the room.

"I'm going to my chambers as well." I tossed my plate into the Zorb hole and headed towards the stairs.

Judas and Alva followed me as Judas said, "I can crash in your place tonight if you'd like. Ming is off to persuade Urral to impregnate her," he said as Ming directed a lewd gesture in our direction making her way to the medical bay.

"I need to get some rest and would really rather be alone tonight." I said as we walked down the stairs. I hoped Les was not already in my chamber waiting. Ansely had joined Judas and Alva and the three of them headed towards Judas' room.

"We'll be watching some old battle holograms if you feel like joining us." Alva said as I walked in the opposite direction.

Les was not in my chambers when I entered and so I attempted to read while I waited for him, but I could not help but let my mind wander to the conversation we had had earlier that evening. I was aghast at the Par's lack of interest or efforts towards peace, and I was intent on learning the Vokkna language. I did not know if my endeavors would do anything to bring about peace, and I did not believe Les had any intention of allowing me to make any real change anyway, but I knew I could not live with myself if I did not at least try.

Les entered my room moments later in nearly a sprint. He was out of breath as he said, "We must go now. Tikk has readied the ship and we are to jump to Hurran immediately." I stood and had just enough time to toss the tablet aside before he grabbed my arm and pulled me along after him down the stairs.

We entered the main docking area and were welcomed by Tikk and Urral, who stood by the humming cargo ship. "Why are we taking this massive thing?" I asked as Les pulled me through the oval entrance to the ship. "It's just the four of us, right?"

"This is the only ship with a full Zorb, and we do not wish to bring unwanted attention to this mission." Tikk was pressing himself into the wall beside me and I could hear the ship gearing up as a Zorb hovered in millions of tiny pieces in the center of the console; I shoved myself into the wall beside my green companion.

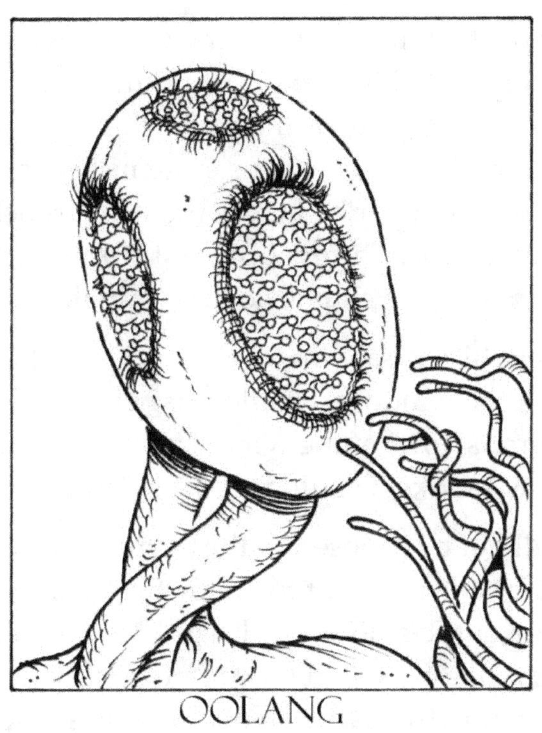
OOLANG

23.

"Oolang will be waiting for us." Les said as the ship leapt onto the Yittar docking area. "The captive is being held nearby and Oolang has guaranteed us an interview with it."

“How are they holding it?” I asked. “From the looks of these things, you can’t exactly put chains around it.”

“We have created a Philex sphere and encased the Vokkna inside it. The trap was laid beneath the Vokkna soil and clamped shut upon the Vokkna as it glided over." Les pushed himself from the wall as we came to a stop. The ship rested on top of the bright green algae covered rocks that covered the planted. The Harllukna resided within the intricate cave systems beneath the surface. Blue sleet whirled across the dangerously beautiful landscape. The ever present storm slammed chunks of ice into the ship's viewing protal.

"Will the ship be safe up here?" I asked as I approached the window. I could not help but flinch, at the thunderous howl of the wind. "How do we get below ground?" As I spoke, I could feel the ship slowly sinking.

"We will not be exposed to the elements for long." Tikk stood beside me. "But the planet is hydrogen based and thus not sufficient for our lungs." He handed me the clear face mask that would ensure my ability to breath and I copied him by placing it over my face. The ship came to a rest and we were engulfed in darkness.

"Are they going to turn on a light?" I reached my hands in front of me and met Tikk's chest. He gripped my fingers as I heard the door to the ship open.

"Do not worry." I could hear humor in his voice. "Oolang will provide light." I had not come into contact or even seen a hologram of a Harlukkna at this point and so did not expect the bright blue creature that waited outside of our ship. Oolang was translucent and glowed from within. Harlukkna are all cartilage except for their bony spines, which are intertwined and can be seen clearly through their pale blue skin. Oolang was considered a handsome Harlukkna, and despite the four craters that made up their face, I could see the aesthetic appeal. As we sunk into the planet Les informed me that the Harllukna are both male and female, so they used the collective pronoun when referring to themselves. The way Oolang embraced Les with obvious love won me over immediately. Tikk was right, Oolang lit up the entire chamber we stood in and I was able to see that we had sunk into a long empty tunnel.

Oolang spread two flanking arms wide and and extended the third towards us. Their body began to shimmer with every shade of blue, and a small band wrapped around the center appendage's wrist produced the words,"My friends."

Oolang flinched, remembering the translator device and then continued. Oolang radiated color as shining appendages sprang into life, and the small translator said, "It has been far too long."

Tikk moved forward to join in the welcoming and I shifted backwards to allow them their moment, but Oolang looked to me and said while reaching for my arm, "You must introduce me to the new species you have found. She is lovely, with skin far more pleasing to touch." The seven thin digits that extended from each appendage were soft, cold, and more adequate for an aquatic atmosphere, and I feared if I returned the searching grasp I would puncture the delicate epidermis.

"Do not fear hurting me." Oolang said as I searched within the craters of their face for a place to rest my gaze, and I notice tiny fibers reaching for me from within the indented sections of Oolang's skull. The translucent skin sparkeled as filaments wrapped around my forearm. "I am far sturdier than I appear."

I reached my hand towards Oolang's face and traced the edge of the dark crater that was directed toward me. I couldn't help but giggle as Oolang's skin flashed neon at my touch.

"Enough of your flirtations," Les had no problem with gripping the Harlukkna's thin skin; he shoved Oolang's hands away from me and turned his friend towards the dark tunnel. "Our business must be conducted quickly and without attracting attention. We will discuss Elinor as we make our way to the prisoner."

I wondered why I had I lost the ability to speak for myself as I followed them.

"Very well." Oolang raised filaments in the air in a submissive manner and led the way.

"You were always the possessive type Les, but I did not believe you would find love with a foreigner."

Les shifted away from me at Oolang's words but he did not argue and Oolang continued. "Tell me Elinor, are you as adept with the Kara as Les informs me?"

I walked between Tikk and Les quietly for a moment not knowing how to reply. I still had little confidence in my abilities as a Kara warrior, but my control of the Kara the previous night was something worth mentioning.

"I don't know what Les has told you, but I am the best in our squad, and have maneuvered the Kara in ways I didn't know were possible." I said.

"Modesty and skill are a fantastic combination in any Kara warrior. Too bad Les was never able to emulate both traits at the same time."

Oolang pulsated light blue rays while Les, Tikk and Urral broke into a deep uproarious laughter. I was pleased to see Les in such a jovial mood and began to join in with their good humor as Oolang continued. "Tell me of your planet of origin Elinor. From what I can tell it must have been very hospitable. On the level of Tralccore even. Les informs me that your species destroyed it--a daunting accomplishment for a fledgling race." Again, I took a moment to collect my thoughts. Hearing my species history put so simply brought new shame to the surface.

"Yes, humans... We were ignorant and thoughtless to say the least. I believe my colony is the last of humanity, and we are eternally thankful to the Par for saving us."

Oolang came to a stop in front of what appeared to be a wall as I finished, "We owe them a great debt."

The tunnel wall fell apart to reveal an opening into a dark room with two Harlukkna standing guard next to what I first took for a small boulder.

"You will certainly have your opportunity for repayment," Oolang said as he led us into the room. Two tall Harlukkna flanked a massive bubble. Each Harlukkna held one of the infamous Harlukkna blades, sheets of steel pulled from the cave walls as long and wide as wings. "If this war is to be restarted you and your fellow Kara warriors will be the main component in it." When Oolang spoke the large mass inside the bubble jerked and began to uncoil. The rock broke apart and vibrated with life. Expanding and swirling in different directions and then rested in a pulsing cloud. A pattern within the pulsations was unmistakable; it was speaking to us.

With a jerk the Vokkna stopped abruptly and its energy was thrust in my direction. The Vokkna then became the tornado of rock I had heard so much about. If the Vokkna had not been confined to the clear Philex sphere we would have been able to hear the wind gusts it formed. The rock formation began to pulsate in patterns again and I searched for understanding.

"It senses the Kara within her. Something it believed long dead." said Oolang as the other two Harlukknan held their blades at ready.

It was clear that despite its captive state and the fact that the Vokkna could not easily kill a Harlukkna, the Vokkna was still an intimidating presence. I could not blame them; to this day I still have a visceral reaction at the sight of a Vokkna. I have learned to live among them in peace, but I will always remember the pain of a Vokkna attack, and always see a part of them as my enemy. The violence of war is a difficult thing to forget even in times of peace.

"It is communicating nonverbally, correct?" I asked as I watched the limited movement of the Vokkna. I was pressed against the wall by this point. The two Harlukkna that held spears stood closest to the captive. A well trained Harlukkna will spin and twist the wide blade through a Vokkna assailant. The only way to physically harm the Vokkna, other than Kara, is to separate or dislodge its millions of pieces. The three Par and Oolang stood slightly behind the blades for this exact reason.

"Correct." Oolang stepped forward and shifted in a fluid dance that calmed the creature. "That is why our species and the Vokkna were able to learn each other's languages so quickly. Trrcck has only been on planet two lunations and we have nearly total communication. Well, we understand each other, but cannot reproduce one another's mother tongue, which is the same case with Parian." He looked to each Par to let the statement sink in and continued, "I have done numerous comprehension practices with a Par translator, and Trrcck appears to understand the language."

"How did you get the LiquiParian into… Trrcck?" I asked with difficulty.

"Through a gas engulfment, similar to the Kara, but not deadly of course," Urral replied.

"How can it see?" I asked.

"It cannot. Valkkarie's sun is harsh and blinding half the rotation and then nearly gone the other, and so the Vokkna evolved without the need for ocular vision. They use sensory deprivation in a similar way to the Harlukkna."

To watch Oolang communicate was like watching a piece of art in motion. I could not take my eyes off the two dancing forms as the Harllukna and Vokkna interacted.

“How can it sense you through the bubble?” I continued my line of questioning.

“The Philex is extremely thin while remaining impenetrable. I can sense Trrcck through it.” Oolang answered with the air of a proud teacher.

“So, this is a language we can also learn." I looked toward Les as I said this. "There were human dialects that used hand movement and gesture in a similar way. It’s just taking the time to understand the meanings."

"Yes, and then you will be able to learn firsthand that the Vokkna view you and all other species as inferior and wish you dead." Les was rigid as he watched the Vokkna pulsating in its prison.

I sighed but could not ignore Les' remark. "Is this true Oolang?”

"The Vokkna's culture is rooted in violence; they do not trust easily. They battle among their own species endlessly; over the most foolish things."

Oolang paused and motioned toward the Vokkna as it became unsettled again. Glowing pale white, Oolang continued. "I forget it can understand me. My apologies, but this is the way my culture views yours."

Oolang was answered with grinding marble and a vertical flutter of dust. "The Vokkna hold beliefs that do not make logical sense to our kind, and the fact that they kill each other over trifling disagreements about these beliefs confounds us to no end."

"Religion." I said as I met Les' eyes.

"You had mentioned some kind of new insight into the Vokkna in your last message," Oolang said also looking towards Les. "Is.... religion... this insight?" There is not motion for religion in the Harlukkna language and so Oolang made a recording of my voice for future use.

"Yes, it is a belief system the humans of the past adhered to, and Elinor's description of the human's struggle with it reminded me of the way you spoke of the Vokkna's internal struggles."

"Religion was a belief system that humans created in order to explain how they came into existence; to explain life." I interjected.

I was met with a confused tilt of the head by Oolang and I became very self-conscious of how absurd all of this was about to sound.

"Like, there was an all knowing, all powerful, human-like thing in the sky that made humans and put them on Earth, our planet, because the being wanted to be entertained or see life unfold or.... I really don't know. It was thousands of years ago when humans truly believed in this rubbish, but I do know that many wars were waged over slight differences in theories."

The room was silent as Oolang turned to communicate with the Vokkna who broke the stillness with its grating response.

"That is strikingly like the Vokkna's culture. Their wars are over the smallest difference in opinion and can wage for generations. It is good to know that your species did eventually grow away from such uneducated beliefs. I wonder if it can be done for the Vokkna?"

"I believe it can." I spoke up before Les had a chance. "Through communication and education, just as you said. If we learn how to teach them, we can change the way all of us live."

"Or they will simply kill us in the process. There is no reasoning with a species like the Vokkna. They only understand force." Les broke in.

"And so that's it? You know there is an opportunity for real communication, and you toss it aside. You would prefer to put our lives at risk instead of even trying for peace. All because you see them as inferior. Your knowledge does not elevate you above them, because you refuse to use it for good. Your actions make you as ignorant as the Vokkna." I stepped forward and everyone recoiled except the Vokkna.

"I agree with Elinor," Oolang said.

"They are right, Les." Tikk stepped in the middle of all of us and stretched his hand out to his commander. The room was thick with tension. We all hovered on the next words Les would utter. "And now that it can understand Parian as well…"

"I know you are right." It was as if he had just lost a long race. "The clear choice is an attempt at peace, but we must prepare for war. The Vokkna will not change their ways so easily."

I could not keep the smile from my lips and was met with a grunt from Les as he shifted uneasily. "You all behave as if I am the savage. Come, it is late, and you have training tomorrow." I allowed my smile to broaden as I followed Tikk into the tunnel.

"If you mean what you say, I will be happy to teach you the Vokkna language, Elinor." Oolang glided to my side.

"I do, when can I return to Hurran? Perhaps tomorrow night?" I spoke loudly to ensure Les heard.

"That would not be rational." Les said over his shoulder. "We will set up a communication line for you and that way your lessons will not interfere with your training. Oolang, till we meet again."

Les and his friend embraced in a mess of color.

"I am truly pleased with our latest encounter." Oolang replied as they released each other; Oolang turned to the rest of us and said, "Soon, my friends."

"Soon," The three males said in unison with me following suit a second later, which I laughed at and was pleased when they joined me.

24.

The next morning training continued as usual. All the Par knew what we had done, but I would have to inform the rest of the humans. I would be contacting Grymm in order to set up a meeting of some kind. Of course, I had to find a way to get in touch with him and that way could not be Les. My first choice was Tikk and so that next evening after Kara training, I found Tikk in the lounge skulking over his device.

"Tikk, would you be able to get me in touch with Oolang?" I leaned against the window and tried to look nonchalant.

"Yes, of course, but I thought Les was planning on opening a line for you." Tikk had not raised his eyes from his tablet.

"I don't know where Les is and I'd really like to contact Oolang tonight. What are you staring at?" I stepped closer to him and he pressed the device to his chest.

"It is an image Kang has sent me. It is a private image." Tikk grinned mischievously.

"Tikk, you scoundrel! How does Kang even have the ability to send you images?" I asked standing akimbo.

"I assigned him a line the day of the banquet so I could send him images of the event, and it made communicating with a shy human easier." If Tikk had the ability to blush he would have at that moment.

"You sly bastard," I said as I gave him numerous small pokes to show the extent of my annoyance. "You are playing favorites and you have not chosen me; I am seriously jealous. Does anyone else have a line?"

"Only Kang.... follow me." He slapped away my hands and led me into the medical room; Urral was busy working on his screen as we walked in.

"I have just been looking over your recent scans Elinor." He said when he saw us. "The fetus is growing at an average rate. You will give birth on schedule, Moon Cycle 1 of next rotation; very exciting." Tikk and I had stopped and both males were staring at me.

"The males of your species really enjoy the process of child birth." I said, and they continued to beam at me, so I motioned Tikk forward with, "The line."

He shook himself and walked towards the back wall which housed storage I had yet to explore. He opened the cabinet and stepped inside. I turned back to find Urral still staring at me with the same large grin on his face.

"Can I help you, Urral?" I asked.

"I apologize for staring Elinor." Urral shifted his gaze to his screen. "I was checking if the fetus had begun to show yet, but I do not think so. There is no problem with this. Most fetuses do not begin to show until the fifth or sixth moon."

"Five to six lunations?" I stepped closer to Urral and he dropped the device. "I am not knowledgeable about pregnancies of any kind. My brother was the last human born on Kepler, but I feel like five to six moon cycles is quite far into the pregnancy."

"What is common for the human anatomy?" Urral asked as Tikk emerged from the cabinet.

"Like I said, I don't know exactly, but sooner than that, I am certain, and a human pregnancy is usually nine lunations. I'm sure this will be different due to the alien sperm and everything, but I want...." I didn't know how to complete that statement, so I changed the subject. "What have you got for me?" I asked Tikk.

"Your own device," He looked at the translucent screen in his hand as if he had forgotten it was there. "I do not know why we have not already given all of you your own for communication."

I took the clear, two deminsional square from his hands and turned it toward my face so it would come to life.

"I guess because none of you have asked for one yet," Tikk continued. "This is a communication tablet that you may keep in your personal belongings. I have created a communication code for you here." He pointed to the five large green numbers projecting from my screen. "You may contact anyone by using their code once it has been embedded into your device. Oolang's line is already embedded, here." He swiped something that I missed, so I pulled the tablet from his clutches.

"I'll play with it when I get to my room. If it's as easy as your reading tablets I'll figure it out quickly." As I spoke Ming entered.

“You will also be able to use this to read and download holograms. It connects to the main chronicle.” Tikk said as Ming approached us.

"I've been looking for you; it’s last meal." She jerked her thumb behind her. "Are you ok?" I pretended to not hear the question.

"I'm starving." I said and headed toward the dining hall.

"El, what’s up? You’ve been MIA all day.” Ming said as she trailed behind me.

I turned on my heels to face her and said, "I am going to learn the Vokkna language. The Harlukkna, Oolang specifically, can teach us. There is a way to negotiate peace…" I continued in a lowered voice as Luke and Shurr passed us. "But it’s going to be tough to get the Par's support. We went to the planet Hurran last night and saw the Vokkan captive."

"You saw one," Ming's hand grasped my arm and her hushed tone matched my own. "And they could communicate with it?"

"Not really, it can understand Parian, but of course can’t speak it, and the same with Harlukkna, but Oolang could fully talk to it. Les has agreed to attend the peace summit; to actually give it a try." Les peeked his head around the opening to the dining hall.

"You need sustenance." Was all he said even though he continued to glare at the two of us.

"I know," I finally said. "We will come in when we are done speaking to each other." I turned back to Ming as he grumbled away. "I got this tablet and a communication line. I'm going to contact Oolang after meal and begin my lessons tonight."

"What did it look like? Can I join?" I turned to see Les peeking around the opening once more.

"I will tell you more after we eat, come to my chambers." I said as an ending to the conversation.

We ate quickly under the watchful eyes of Les and the rest of the Par. I knew Tikk and Urral had gone running to Les to inform him of my request. I decided to skip the middle man in my next move, so turned to him mid chew and asked, "Would you be able to get me a meeting with Grymmig sometime soon, or his communication code so I can set it up myself?"

He nearly choked on his Yurrlu, and when he did not answer me after he had regained his composure I asked again.

"When did you get a comm code?" was his only reply.

"Is that kind of like an identification number that you can contact people with?" Ming asked. "I want one of those."

"Are we getting identification numbers?" Bo chimed in from across the table.

"I do not know what an identification number is, but you all already have been given comm codes." Shurr said disgruntled at the disruption of his last meal of the day.

"Who gave you a comm code?" Les turned so that he was very close to my ear and had lowered his voice so that I had to strain to hear. "If you wish to communicate with anyone you may do so through me."

"No, I do not. You were there when Oolang and I discussed my language lessons." I replied in a regular volume. "And besides, the things I wish to talk with Grymmig about do not concern you."

"Come with me now." Les stood and took hold of my arm.

"Are you seriously touching me right now?" I exclaimed and the room went silent. Les did not release my arm so I jerked it free and stood facing him. "I will do as I want and speak with whom I want. I can get in touch with Grymmig without you."

"Stop being foolish. You would not even know where to start." At that point he was correct, but I was angry enough to do anything, so instead of responding I ran out of the room, down the stairs, and into the open night.

Les chased me of course, and his long legs enabled him to catch me a short distance from the arena. "Why are you running? What are you trying to accomplish with this?" He demanded, but I was just as confused by my actions as he was.

"I don't know," I replied between gulps for air. "I was angry and needed to get away from you. The way you smell is... aggravating." I said as my nostrils filled with his scent yet again.

"Please, give Grymmig my communication code. Nothing will interfere with training, and if the Vokkna are as worthless a cause as you believe, where is the harm? Allow me to at least try and fail." I had regained my composure by the end.

"Very well." He said. "Have your meeting; it will amount to nothing." He walked past me into the night.

"Where are you going?" I called after him.

"I need the cool air on my skin." He did not turn to face me. "Unless you need me to return to your chambers with you."

"No… no, that will not be necessary." I turned and stormed inside before I could catch a whiff of him on the breeze. When I arrived at my chamber Ming was already waiting for me. Judas was sitting beside her with his arms crossed.

"Do I get told everything last now?" He said as I entered the room. They both sat on my bed, so I made my way to the opposite wall and another one folded out for me to rest on.

"Did people ever share anything with you before?" I asked mimicking his body language. "You're not exactly the empathetic type." I looked to Ming and upon noting she held my newly appointed tablet said, "Toss it over."

"Did Les agree to put you in touch with Grymmig?" She slung the clear device towards me, and I nearly lost it as it flew towards me. "I can't even get it to light up like the others," She said, but as I faced the device towards me it came to life. I had a small blue notification that I tapped.

"This kind must be assigned to an individual owner like ours used to be. I don't know how I feel about the lack of a case or outer border. I feel like I will lose this thing if it's not constantly lighting up." I giggled to myself as a picture of Oolang, along with a message flashed onto my screen. "He has asked me to contact him tomorrow evening. I wonder what time it is on Hurran right now, or if there is any kind of time difference between Sharron and Yitar." I tossed the tablet on the bed and leaned against the wall.

"So, what's with the change of heart?" Judas asked. "You meet one Vokkna captive and suddenly you switch alliances." He wore his classic look of disapproval.

"This is why people don't come to you directly with their problems." I rolled my eyes but answered his question as much for myself as for their benefit. "I haven't switched sides and I still support the Par completely. They saved us... and compared to the Vokkna they are cute and cuddly, but I don't feel as one sided about the whole thing anymore. The Vokkna are living creatures even though they are unlike anything I have ever encountered, and we can't treat them like mindless monsters that need to be destroyed."

"But you said you couldn't actually communicate with it." Ming interjected.

"I couldn't but Oolang could. They had a conversation. That means the Vokkna captive made an effort to learn the Harlukkna language; that's more than the Par have ever done. They just wrote it off immediately. The entire trip was Les trying to prove a point to me, which of course failed, but they did seem to come around at the end. They are at least now willing to attend the peace summit with some amount of legitimate aim towards peace. At least that's what they made it seem like last night in front of Oolang." I shrugged.

"The Harlukkna, right, is their skin really thinner than ours?" Judas asked and leaned into the conversation. He was not interested in the idea of creating peace with creatures he had already written off as enemies, but the chance of encountering another humanoid species enticed him as much as it did the rest of us.

"Here," I said as I stood with the tablet and made room between them to sit. They looked over my shoulders to see the image of Oolang that appeared beside his message.

"He looks like glowing jelly." Ming was the first to speak. "Did you get to touch him?"

"Only for a second but they felt crazy soft and squishy." I laughed to myself. "And they don't have a gender. So, no he or she, only they, them, their. Because they are both genders."

"Do you think we will get a chance to meet him… it… them," Judas stumbled on the new pronouns. There had been humans with idintifications like this on Earth, but none in our camp that we knew of. "Before the Peace Summit? Once we're there we'll be too busy Kara-ing a bunch of Vokkna ass holes to get a real introduction." Judas was clearly excited with the idea of using his new weapon for something other than training. He and Ming had grown much more competent over the passing weeks and we would all grow stronger through the coming moon cycles. I too wanted to use the new skills I had honed, but a part of me feared the coming altercation and this fear fueled my desire to make contact with the Vokkna.

"Hopefully there will be no need to Kara anybody, and I don't know. We might have to wait till the summit. I mean… well, no, they can leave their caves since Oolang fought with the Par before. They could come here and meet everyone." I said.

"They live in caves?" Ming asked

"There is a massive storm the size of Kepler raging across the planet that makes living above ground impossible. Only that crazy healthy bacteria we eat grows above the surface. You really should pay attention during our lessons, Ming." I nudged her with my elbow, and she stood.

"I'm always exhausted by the time we're in there and Shurr has the most monotone voice I have ever heard. I don't know how any of us are expected to pay attention. They should let Urral do the lectures." She stared off into space with a teenage gleam in her eyes. "His throaty voice would keep my attention."

"If this is where the conversation is heading, I'm going to my chambers." Judas stood and made his way to the exit.

"Both of you get out of here. I'm tired and unlike Ming I like to stay conscious during the lesson and so need my rest." I lay out on my bed as they left the room, but I did not drift into sleep the way I had originally hoped. Instead I fantasized about my meeting with Grymmig and how angry it would make Les, and how the idea of angering him was as much a part of the enjoyment of the action as actually accomplishing my goal.

25.

Let's bounce forward a lunation. I remember waking up one morning three ticks before the early siren was due to sound. I hate that feeling. Lying in bed, knowing you will not be able to sleep any longer, but having just enough time left to think about how much you would enjoy staying within the warmth of your bed.

I kicked the blanket off and made my way outside for the morning cardio. I had been completing the required morning routine with ease lately and had started adding extra strength routines of my own invention to push myself harder. I found the fetus inside of me had made me capable of more, but also required more nutrients and so when it came time for first meal, I consumed my weight in left over Juwakkwon beast.

"Careful, El, you'll make yourself sick." Ming said. I made guttural noises as she quietly sipped her Yurrlu.

I came up for air and said, "I'm starving and need to make it through the days lectures without a rumbly tummy. Les gets all stressed and will make me visit Urral again."

Ming added, "I know, and that always gets Shurr to end his lecture early, which means we get to start Kara training early, then an early weight session followed by an early start to personal time." We both nodded at our desire for more time to ourselves, or at least some time to explore the planet we were supposed to be willing to die for. Other than morning cardio we were not permitted to enter the large city of Sharron. Les said it was best we keep our distance from the populace until we are fully in control of our Kara.

"What does he think is happening?" Ming asked.

"Urral told me that when a fetus gives energy to the mother there's a sound." I smiled at Ming's squinched nose and continued. "A grumbling sound that's a louder version of our stomachs growling when we're hungry. Les is worried that I'm not eating enough." We both laughed at that.

"You eat more than any creature I have ever seen." Ming threw her head back and snorted. "I truly believe if the situation occurred you would have zero issue cutting my ass up and eating me raw."

"I believe you are right." I said. "Your rump is deliciously meaty, but these arms," I lifted her right wrist into the air and began tickling her under her arm pit while teasing, "These arms are spindly and tough. They will not do for a meal. I'll have to boil them in a broth."

Ming attempted to pull from my grasp, but I held tight. We had both grown stronger and more defined. Ming was suddenly crashing to the floor with me tumbling on top of her, just as Grymmig and Les entered the room.

"It is good to see that you are keeping morale light." Grymmig said as he glared down at Ming and me. His eyes were filled with lust, but it was never my body Grymmig desired. Grymmig got off on power.

"What brings you to our humble abode?" I straightened myself as I spoke.

"Les informed me of your interest in speaking with me. I was hoping to steal you away for a short period of time. I also have something I would like to discuss with you." He answered in quick staccatos, like nails in my brain.

His smile was as genuine as a Juwakkwon beast's toothy grin right before it pounces on your face and pulls your nasal cavity out through your mouth with its two long middle canines.

"Of course,... umm... we are about to have lessons." I glanced toward Les who was already watching me.

"You can spare half a fraction to listen to what Grymmig has to say." He said.

"And to discuss my issues as well," I spoke louder than intended and over corrected by whispering, "Shall we speak in the lounge?" I left the room and made my way down the hall before I got an answer.

"What was it you wished to ask of me, Elinor?" The way Grymmig said my name made it sound dirty. "Les made it seem as if you were quite adamant we speak." He took a seat in one of the cushions that he summoned from the room; his black skin covered in black Philex made him a blot on the pristine setting. I remained standing.

"I want you to set aside a sum of money to be used towards furthering our understanding of the Vokkna language and culture. I wish to return to Hurran at least three times a lunation in order to stay abreast of any further knowledge or advances in communication, and to learn the Vokkna language. I believe the Vokkna want to talk to us as much as we want to talk to them." I paused and Grymmig's lips twitched upward at the corners. "Perhaps more even," I added.

"Sadly, that is not possible at this time." His features had returned to their emotionless state. "I have just spent a large sum of our funds on a new propaganda campaign. We need to bring awareness to our cause and help the public learn who you are and how you are going to save us all from the Vokkna threat."

“Propaganda…” It was obvious that our cultures had different connotations in regard to the word. "What are you going to do?"

"Our culture has a vast array of media, and our citizens have a great desire to be informed on every subject that could affect them personally. They even care about subjects that have nothing to do with them at all because they have become convinced that it does in fact affect them." He smiled with self-awareness. I was impressed by his ability to see his own ruthlessness, but it did not endear me to him in any way. So sure of my inferiority due to my sex, Grymmig had allowed his guard to drop.

"And what was it you came here to ask of me," I said even though I already knew the answer.

"You know exactly what I want of you, and of your

fellow warriors, but you are the only one I need to speak with. You are the leader. By shear happenstance you are the voice of the Par army. An alien female is the only hope for Par-kind, and it is my job to get the populace to love you, and to support you financially." I knew my only option, and Grymmig was waiting for me to offer it to him.

"Allow me to visit Hurran a few times a lunation and if we are able to have a legitimate discussion about peace with the Vokkna you must allow the Par to take part in that discussion; even if the summit ends in war we will have at least tried to come to an alliance. If you give me that I will do whatever kind of propaganda you ask of me, and I will encourage my squad to do the same."

He got what he wanted, and it cost him very little in the end, but I had permission to do as I pleased from the only Par superior to Les. The war would happen. There was no stopping it now, and I would take a leading role in the death of thousands of innocent lives, but at that moment I believed I was making a stand for my beliefs.

"Granted." Grymmig said as he stood and moved toward me. He pulled his tablet from a compartment in his suit.

"Here," He faced the screen upwards between us. "Make your statement again and it will become official."

"Are you going to record me?" I asked as I craned my neck to see Grymmig's device.

He raised it so the screen was just out of view and said, "Yes, I will send it to my headquarters so that it may be filed away in case we ever need to return to it again. It is never good to have misunderstandings in these matters."

"Of course." I rested in an akimbo position. "Can you send me a copy? I can give you my communi… comm code."

"Yes, that will be just fine." He spoke to me like a mother commends her child for outsmarting her. I repeated our agreement and then Grymmig tucked the tablet back into his chest.

I knew that if I could get ahold of that device, I could destroy the Par standing before me, but also knew I could do nothing about it at the moment so I let the matter rest until a time when my power was stronger.

***

Acrobatic weight routines were always a good way to lose myself and turn off my thoughts for a while. We would spend two fractions a day with our bodies constantly in motion, leaping across the arena floor as we dodged yellow and purple weight spheres while catching the green and blue. Unbeknownst to us, our trainers had taken it easy on us at first. Purposefully throwing the ball to the side or calling out as they threw one, we needed to catch. Now, six lunations in, we left every session bruised and sore, barely able to make it to our chambers where we either slept or stared at the wall moving as little as possible. The evening after I had spoken with Grymmig was spent in just that fashion. Unable to sleep and unable to lift my reading tablet, I lay on my bed and contemplated the agreement I had just made with the one Par I should not be making agreements with.

Depending on how much Yurrlu we consumed during our session, and how hard we had pushed ourselves, it took the Kara anywhere from a couple of moments to the entire night to renew, but we were always fully recuperated by morning so there was never an excuse to miss the next day's morning cardio. That said, last meal had become more of a silent ordeal since the weight sessions had grown more intense.

That evening, I ate silently beside Alva and found myself enjoying the noiseless company of my fellow warriors. I had to force myself to break the silence to inform them of my foolish decision.

"I spoke with Grymmig earlier today, and he wants us to start doing propaganda appearances and things." I looked around at the confused faces of my comrades.

“More explanation is necessary,” Luke cocked his head and continued to chug his fourth cup of Yurrlu.

"I'm assuming they want us to make some live appearances and answer some questions; introduce ourselves to the population and let them know we have their best interest in mind. It is kind of weird to think about going to war for a bunch of total strangers. I'm sure it's weird for them as well." I was met with the sound of gulping.

"If it means we can get out of this arena for a day, I'm down" Odelia was the first to speak up and I was thankful for the support.

"It would be nice to actually see some real Par – the ones that live on this planet and are really depending on us. The space guys and Grymm cannot be the basic model of Par." Bo said, and the rest of the table appeared to be in agreement.

"Did he actually use the word propaganda?" Alva asked me.

"He literally used it," I replied. "And from what he said they seem to have a pretty legitimate media empire here." I looked around as if I was searching for the media.

"Where?" Alva said also searching the air around her.

"Of course, we haven't been allowed to follow the media," Judas shouted from across the room. "I'm sure they're saying all kinds of stuff about us and the war. That's probably why Grymm wants us to start doing public appearances suddenly. Just the other day Les said we weren't safe enough to be around the public. Now we're going on public appearances to promote our likability… but I am also willing to do just about anything to get a day away from here."

Our bodies were in their peek physical shape, but our minds were jelly. Everything had started so quickly and now that things were beginning to settle, we all felt a bit trapped.

"Ok, I guess we just wait for instructions." I said.

"Like always." Alva shrugged between slurps.

We sat in silence for another few ticks before Ansley said, "Do we all get communication codes?"

Ming avoided my stare and said, "How would I not tell them. I want one too. I don't even know who I would contact, maybe you." We both smiled.

"I'm all for it," I said, "Tikk can get you one, just ask." I stuffed the last of my food in my mouth and shuffled out the door. I just remembered that I was supposed to contact Oolang.

I was greeted by a tiny blue light flashing on the tablet when I entered my chamber. It was the recording of Grymmig and or arrangement. I listened to it until the sound of my own voice forced me to shut it off. I found the message from Oolang and searched for the button that would allow me to contact him. I eventually held my finger down on Oolnag's image until the entire screen came to life. My screen hummed and glowed blue as the large image of Oolang took up my field of vision. Then everything went silent and the image came to life.

"Elinor, I am glad to see you, and am very excited to begin our lessons."

As Oolang's arms moved and the color morphed I became aware that we were now live, and my hands shot towards my unkept hair.

"I didn't realize you guys communicated with video," I said to fill the silence.

"Of course, the Harlukkna communicate entirely through non-verbal movements and pigment shifts, and even though the Par use verbal language to express themselves the Harlukkna prefer to have a visual representation of the being we are conversing with,"

Oolang said by blinking between grey and sky blue.

"I have just received permission from Grymmig to visit Hurran a few times a lunation to keep up with what you are doing."

"I am pleased with this news, but I hope the effort was not inconvenient for you." Oolang flashed white with excitement. "Now, are you ready for your first lesson in Vokkna?"

And so, began my introduction to the visual language of the Vokkna. Oolang conducted the lessons with Trrcck and so I was able to learn a language while getting to know my new found enemy. Both the Vokkna and Harlukkna languages are intricate and incredibly nuanced. One false move and the entire meaning is changed. I am still learning new forms of communication to this day, but I am proud to say that I was able to carry on a conversation with Trrcck by the end of one lunation, but I must give the majority of the credit to my teacher.

I ended the night lying in my bed and contemplating the agreement I had made with Grymmig. I listened to our binding contract numerous times and with every moment I grew more frustrated with myself. I had actually said, "Any propaganda you want

I felt myself growing frustrated and then nauseous. I sighed to emit my built-up Kara, but then I decided to try to fly. I focused all my attention to the back of my body. I envisioned my Kara pushing from my back and lifting me off my bed, and that is exactly what happened. The white ceiling rushed towards my face faster than I could put my hands up and I was knocked senseless right before my body plummeted back to the space on the floor where my bed had once been.

26.

My fall was loud enough to draw the attention of the entire fourth floor. Soon I was surrounded by Ming, Judas, Ansely, and Alva, all wondering what happened as they looked down at my crumpled form.

"You ok, El?" Judas helped me sit up.

"Yes... I just… I just Kara-ed my face to the ceiling." I cupped my nose and forehead with my hands, but it was my pride that hurt the most. Then I regained my composure, "I flew!" I stood up and everything went white as Ming pushed me back down by the shoulders.

"Sounds to me like you fell." She said with a laugh as a bed appeared along the other wall and I sat down.

Alva shouted, "I'm going to get Urral. You know Les is going to freak when he finds out that the body carrying his future child made that noise." She rushed out of the room as Innc and Les came running in.

"See." We could hear her say from the hall.

"What happened here?" Les demanded.

"She disintegrated her bed." Judas said, annoyed at the presence of the two large males in the already crowded room.

"And flew, supposedly." Ming added.

"Not supposedly," I looked up at Les. I could not help but smile at how upset he was.

"I used my Kara to push myself off the bed. I used a

bit too much force and forgot about the whole ceiling thing, but I definitely defied gravity for a few seconds there, and I think I can do it again."

I started to stand and Les kneeled to help me. "A bit more control and head room would help, but I can for sure do it, and I didn't even need you."

"If you levitated the way you say that would indicate a high level of concentration." Les said as he helped stabilize me. "It is possible to use the Kara to levitate for small amounts of time and space, because one must always think of what is below or fatalities will be certain, but I believe you did as you say." Les grasped my shoulders and gave me a quick jolt. "This is spectacular Elinor. You are moving to the next level of your training. Now you must go to the medical chamber for a scan to ensure the child was not affected." We all groaned in unison.

"Seriously, I'm fine." I grabbed his wrists and lifted them from my shoulders. "For now, I just want to go back to bed. The baby is fine." Les nodded and everyone exited my chamber.

I did not sleep well that night, or any night the next lunation. Oolang and I continued our lessons and I was kept informed of their progress with the Vokkna regarding the impending summit, but despite being kept in the loop I felt as if I had no power over the situation, and that Oolang had already given in to the impending war.

Grymmig was even worse. Every day I was met with

a message of some kind creating a schedule of fund raisers and meet and greets. Our first big event was creeping closer and I was not looking forward to the time away from the arena the way my fellow warriors were. Being away from the arena meant no structure, and lack of structure meant more opportunity for Les to be near me, touching me and wafting his scent in my direction. At least at the arena he was busy and away from me for most of the day. I had been training primarily alone the past few turns and had been reveling in my isolation, but, if anything, my attraction for Les had grown stronger with time.

On a day, like most of the others, we were escorted outside when we began Kara training, and we were greeted by a massive slab of Philex laid out along the length of the arena.

"That's the biggest pillow I've ever seen," Talbot said as we rounded the corner.

"Are we having a cuddle party?" Ming added.

"We are moving on to the next level of training." Shurr turned to lean against the mat and made a slight indention with his large form in the soft material. "Elinor has shown that you are more advanced than we assumed, and due to to our lack of time a quickening of pace seems necessary."

The peace summit was a little over three moon cycles away at this point, and although the squad never looked better, we still had much to learn. Our cardio was on point, but the majority of us, me included, still had difficulty controlling the amount of Kara released at one given moment.

"I'll go first." My hand shot into the air as I spoke and I was forced into a flashback of my childhood, and practice rooms where I thrived on besting my peers.

“Here,” Les said and tossed me by my waist onto the high mat of Philex that reached well above his head.

"And you claim to be worried about my safety." I stood and adjusted myself as the mat indented where ever I placed my foot. I was assured that my inevitable fall from the sky would not be painful.

"When you are ready Elinor." Shurr peaked over the edge of the Philex, as everyone backed up in order to see my attempt.

"Should I start from a laying down position?" I made a move to lay flat on my stomach.

"It is up to you.” Shurr replied in his usual educator tone. "You could attempt to push the Kara through your feet and propel yourself that way, but that is a smaller surface and so harder to get enough momentum, but also remember that your feet are constantly expressing Kara, and so are more prone to this kind of action."

I chose to stay on my feet. At least that way I might not land on my face. It wasn't difficult to form the Kara. It had been on the cusp of formation all day, and with the pressure of Les' hands on my hips a rush of fresh adrenalin pulsed through my veins. I had to control it; this is my body, and I was learning to control my power.

A soft green mist pushed forth from the pores along my feet and palms and I slowly rose above the mat. A shot of excitement surged across my body and a wave of emerald fog crashed against the Philex as I flew into the air. I could not stop the cry of elation that escaped my lips as I climbed higher into the sky. I could hear the ruckus below as human and Par began to scatter to catch me if I happened to fly beyond the padded area, but I had gone far more up than over and landed fairly close to the place I had started.

I was giddy with the joy of something new, as Judas scrambled onto the mat half wanting to make sure I was ok and half as a way of making it clear that he was next.

"You were so high up, El!" I could see his Kara on the edge of his eyes and slid off the mat before his excitement got the best of him.

Shurr edged close to the mat and began giving Judas pointers as I hurried back to where the rest of the group stood.

"We need to record these. You should have seen yourself." Ming and Alva were having a grand time imitating my screech. "We have to be able to relive the humiliation later."

"Did anyone bring their device?" I looked around as everyone shook their heads. I was reminded of a time when not one of us would have been without some kind of communication device back on Kepler.

"I have one." Les pulled his tablet from the pocket of his Philex suit. I had not noticed he had been wearing the more formal full suit until that point.

"Why the full suit today? Did you go somewhere?" I eased closer to him as Ansely took the tablet from his hand and began to film and criticize Judas as he lay floundering on the mat trying to shoot Kara from both hands at the same time.

"I had the final scheduling meeting with Grymmig. We will be going over the propaganda schedule tomorrow during our lesson." He leaned closer and I was forced to breath him in. "I do not understand why you agreed to his terms. You get very little out of the bargain, and what you do get will amount to nothing."

"Do you take the time to consider exactly what will upset me before you speak?" I glared up at him and could see his eyes flinch in pain. “Because if so, you are doing spectacular."

I turned and watched as Ansley tossed Odelia the tablet and climbed onto the mat as Judas stumbled off.

"We should have at least two of these. It's wasteful for most of us to be standing around watching while only one person trains," I said as I crossed my arms and turned my back to him.

"I'm going to go for a run. Work on some Kara techniques on my own." I began to jog toward the crystal blue lake where we had first discussed religion.

"This is not something you can do alone." Les was running beside me. "I know you want to work on propulsion more, and I also believe you are right about needing another Philex mat. You cannot work on something that flings you through the air by."

"I don't need you." I kept a steady pace and he matched it. "But I would like your help. I hear you were one of the best." I glanced at him without moving my head, but he caught me anyway.

"I was the best," There was no bravado in his voice, just the statement of fact, like always. It was easy to put ego into his words when it was not there.

I stopped myself from making assumptions as he said, "But I believe you will soon take that title from me."

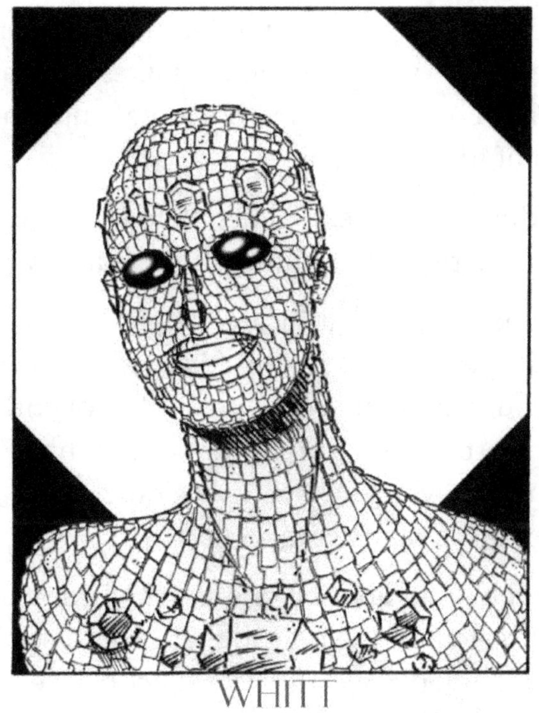

WHITT

27.

A new Philex mat arrived five turns later, but we did not get to properly enjoy it due to our first propaganda appearance. I also received a self-aggrandizing message from Grymmig making it painfully clear that he was responsible for our new mat, and I was reminded once more of the fact that Les and Grymmig communicated daily.

Les and I had begun to train on the mat together in private during the evenings. The night before our second mat was to arrive Les was complaining, "Grymmig is incessant and every suggestion he makes is completely absurd," I hovered above the Philex mat enjoying the distraction of his angry voice.

"What does he suggest?" I began to focus on my hands and was projected higher into the air by the force.

"He wants to make duplicates of you." My concentration was cracked, and I landed on the soft mat. "Not just you, but all of you, which I do not entirely disagree with, but he is so ignorant of anything but business; he believes everything is a quick fix. Duplication takes many rotations."

"Are you talking about cloning us? Making exact replicas?" I rested on the mat so that I could see his ebony eyes as they angled towards me, reflecting the two moons over my shoulder.

"Yes, and the process is not easy. I don't know what kind of education he received but anyone with a farthing of knowledge about duplication knows your reproductions would all have to be produced, allowed to mature, birthed, and then given time to age." He looked past me. "He has even mentioned our offspring. As if he had any say in the future of our child."

"He's not to touch any child of mine. I only agreed to help him at all because I got something out of it. When this war is over so is my relationship with Grymm. I look forward to the day I never see him again." My body surged with Kara, and I felt the release as I floated away from Les' magenta head.

"You speak with such confidence." Les laughed as I practiced spinning in the air. An incredibly difficult task that consists of shifting my focus from one body part to another and making sure the proper body part was facing down.

"Because I have no idea what I'm talking about." I was now admiring the stars, using the bottoms of my feet to project myself horizontally across the mat. "We haven't even begun to fight, so I am free to have all the confidence in the universe. I don't know fear because I have not experienced war."

"I appreciate your ability to recognize that in yourself." He said as he peered over the mat at me. We were really getting good at the communication thing. "For my part, I am terrified, and I do not know how I can ensure your safety on the battlefield or with Grymmig." I allowed myself one quick shot into the atmosphere before I joined him back on the ground.

I had become obsessed with flight. Every moment spent in the air was pure joy for me. Isolated, floating through an atmosphere that did not naturally support me created a sense of calm, but I was in the minority. Odelia for instance had no interest or ability when it came to flight. She detested the feeling of weightlessness and refused any further attempts after her first crash. Talbot and Luke were both equal to my levitation ability and as prone to solitude as myself, so I started to believe flight and loners went together.

Odelia, Ansley, and Judas focused instead on forming Kara walls, which required just as much concentration and skill. The Par would set up Philex obstacles for them to practice making barriers of Kara around. We grew bored with this activity after the first day and instead created a game. The squad would suit up in full Philex while Odelia and whoever else desired to be the chasers, remained in Kara gear. We would start at one end of the arena and try to run to the other side before they could wall us in. I would screech as Ming attempted to use me as a decoy for her own escape across the long room. Despite our Philex suites the Kara was a formidable barrier and we could not help but backpedal and panic as our pursuers sprinted closer, trailing the colorful, deadly mist behind them, but our shrieks were filled with excitement. We played like children whose parents had forgotten to warn them of the dangers of fire. The multicolored fog would float to the ceiling and mingle with the echoes of our laughter.

We were all beginning to form personal strengths, like Judas with his Kara spheres. He would push Kara from every pore along his torso and arms, forming a large ball of bright white mist so thick that it hung in the air like floating water. Runn claimed this as his favorite Kara skill due to its ability to take out up to twenty Vokkna at a time when flung and burst in the proper way, but it drained Judas and left him completely helpless. Since his new-found skill was so draining Judas began to shadow me during cardio work in the mornings. He pushed himself to the brink from the first step and then was unable to keep up after the second length. He would come stomping up to the dinning chamber declaring my freakish ability to run was linked to the creature forming inside of my uterus.

Besides the random outburst of anger and blame, my physical condition did not come up. By the fifth month, a small bulge had formed at the base of my abdomen, but that was the only sign that I was any different from the rest of my crew. I on the other hand could not stop thinking of the life forming inside of my body. If it was not the constant hunger causing me anguish it was Les' persistent need to know how I was doing.

As Judas and I finished our run the day of our first propaganda appearance Les pounced on us with two containers of Yurrlu. "You appear to be hindered in some way." He said as he thrust both containers at me.

I handed one to Judas and said, "I was just slowing down so we could finish together. As usual, I'm fine." Judas chugged down the Yurrlu without taking his eyes off Les. The two most prominent men in my life hated each other.

"When do we head out?" Judas motioned as if he was going to hand the empty jar back to Les and chuckled to himself when he was met with four upturned nostrils; Par are the best creatures in the universe when it comes to expressing disdain. No other species can match them in quiet loathing.

"What are we expected to do at this thing anyway? No one has mentioned anything but when and where." Judas continued his questioning. Les had taken my jar, which was more an act of hostility toward Judas than an act of kindness towards me and was leading us up the stairs.

"That is because there is no need for you to do anything but be present." Les said. "Grymmig and his media team will want to do all the talking. You are purely props." Les took my arm as we reached the fourth floor and pulled me aside as Judas walked away. "Your role is extremely important Elinor. I know that you and the other humans are not able to see signs of your pregnancy at this point, but the Par will."

He caressed my lower abdomen and I stepped back. "It is here." He said as his hand reached for the small bump and I could not help but simper. "They will know immediately, and Grymmig… I believe it will be best for us to appear mated at the rallies." And his fingers were gone, and my skin was left bare and cold. "You do not have to be satisfied with your circumstances in private, but I do expect you to behave accordingly in public." I was pushed backward by the force of his change in demeanor.

"I get it, put on a happy face for the masses. Human culture and Par culture are very similar in this fashion. I know how to fake it." I turned into an empty facility room and undressed.

"Elinor, I do not want your pleasure to be false." He had entered the room as I stood in the orange haze of the cleansing light. "How can I make your pleasure genuine?"

"By getting out of here and letting me get ready." I fidgeted in my nakedness despite our familiarity.

"Then let us have a private meeting tonight. When we have returned from the rally."

"Yes, of course, I'll see you for our night practice at the mat, right?" The light was fading in and out as Les paced the room "You need a cleanse yourself."

We both smiled at my observation. "I also need to change my Philex pattern," He said as he glanced down at himself awkwardly and added, "But first I want to ask… I want us to meet in my room, or in your room; not for training but to speak, to speak about us and the child. I feel that you use training to escape personal conversation."

I flinched at his accuracy. I nodded and stepped out of the dying light as he asked, “Tonight, in your room after last meal?“

"Your room.” I said as I pointed at him and I circled away from his tilted form. "Now go clean yourself." I made a beeline for my chamber where my Philex material and hair detangler were waiting.

The squad was cleaned and looking their finest for our first public appearance. We had all donned the classic full body Philex suit.

"Great minds think alike,” Bo said as he entered the cargo ship and was met with grunts of agreement and rolled eyes. We were all still terrified of accidentally killing a random Par civilian with a burst of unexpected Kara, and so covered as much of our bodies as possible.

Les, Tikk, and Shurr were the only Par joining us.

Grymmig said it was best to keep the attention on the Kara warriors, and that the public had no interest in trainers. Les and Shurr were only allowed on stage because of their past warrior status, and the fame they had earned in prior battles. Tikk was along for the ride and was too busy primping Kang to pay attention to the fact that Grymmig did not want him there.

We arrived in Sharron early. "Do we get to do stuff? Put on a show?" Ansley asked as she examined the large white stage we were to stand on during the event.

This was our first time in the streets of Sharron. I had run in the dry, black hills that surrounded the city many times, but had never broken the barrier that separated the vast sandy country side from the white, urban landscape. The streets of Sharron, unlike those we saw in Typpyton during the banquet, were onyx, spotless, and empty. I had not become aware of the mass transportation that every Par resident was required to use. I had assumed everyone used transport ships to get around the way we did.

We had leapt from the cargo hold of the arena straight to a paved court yard in the middle of the city. Zorb tech was and is free, clean energy, but Grymmig wanted the populace to pay for mass transit that cost him nothing, and so he left the free part out. As soon as we exited the ship it leapt back into the safety of the sealed cargo hold.

Soaring buildings that appeared to be carved out of chalk surrounded the black, open area where we stood. The stage also appeared to be formed from thick chalk but was smooth and cool to the touch. I craned my neck to see the top of the towering structure that loomed behind me.

"The Capital," I heard Les' voice. "Sharronn is the civil hub of Qualittia. Typpyton is bureaucrats and Sharronn is the public. When the war with Valkkari began Sharronn was the first city to begin enlisting warriors. Now the Par of Sharronn are the most adamant about making peace with the Vokkna. That is why their support is most important for our cause."

"So, we are about to promote going to war to the Par who do not in fact want to go to war." I angled my head like the confused animal I was.

"You will change their minds, Elinor. We will show them that war is the only answer." Les spoke with pride.

"But I don't even believe that." I spat back. "If you had allowed me to go back to Hurran at some point in the last lunation I could have worked towards my real goal. I will not stand by while you bullshit these Par. You must give them the truth. There is a chance for peace. War is the last option, not the only option."

"You will most definitely stand by." The sound of Grymmig's voice made my Kara churn. "As per our agreement, you will stand on that stage, smile at the crowd, and keep your mouth shut." His unblinking eyes bore into me and I chose to remain silent.

"We are to wait in the Capital until Whitt announces you." Les was at my elbow.

“Whitt?” I asked as I allowed him to lead me away from Grymmig's menacing glare.

"She is Grymm's daughter, and the head of Mass Media on Qualittia.” Les explained as we walked toward the capital building. “She will be making the rounds with us to all the rallies. She is the most highly trained in commercial jargon. If anyone can sell this war to the Par of Sharronn it will be her."

"That's a pretty high position for a seemingly useless female." I said. We now stood in the massive white lobby of the capitol.

"She is an exception like yourself." Les grinned at the statement he believed to be a compliment.

"Or we are both just as capable as every other female and were simply lucky enough to be placed in circumstances that allowed growth." Our impassioned looks collided, but our discussion on gender was interrupted by Whitt’s appearance.

"Kara warriors," The petite, maroon, feminine figure of Whitt fluttered into the room. Her jeweled chest caught the light and my eyes were drawn to the blue and green coruscate jewels that made up most of her upper body. "It is a pleasure to officially meet you." She addressed the room and then caught my eye directly. "Eliinnorr," She took her time with the name, "I am excited to get to know you better during our time together."

“Yea… sure,” I said as Ming, Judas, and Alva shuffled closer. The rest of my squad lingered apprehensively near the windows. The Par were beginning to congregate outside. We had never seen so many; had not considered what thousands of Par would look like and how they would react to our small band of aliens.

I asked Whitt, "What do you need us to do?"

"Just stand tall and look proud. You should be proud, all of you. You are going to save the planet from enslavement, or worse, and this is not even your planet. You are true heroes. The Par are indebted to you," Whitt said and I immediately understood why she oversaw media. I opposed her cause but was desperate to please the tiny magenta creature. It was her face; her sincerity that could not be taught. She was a professional in every form of the word.

"We are not allowed to speak?" Odelia appeared as displeased with the idea as I was.

"Do you have something you wish to say?" Whitt's voice dripped with concern. Odelia took a step back and turned as red as Whitt. "Nothing in particular... I just thought that was what they all came here for... to get to know us."

"They came here for the assurance that their tax money is being spent in a manner they support. The Par of Sharronn are not supportive of the sacrifices you are making for us. They would rather spend funds and resources on negotiations with the Vokkna. They must be educated. It will be best for my team and I to do the talking for now. Perhaps after your support has grown you will have the opportunity to speak on a more personal level with the population."

I decided at that moment that she would not speak for me, and she did not have to listen or agree, but she would allow it.

"Let's get started." Whitt said as she turned on her heel and sauntered out of the building, which had the first Philex door I had seen. A small hole formed in the middle of the white wall and grew to allow her delicate form to slide through with only the slightest line of sunlight haloed around her.

When we initially made our way through the cavity of alabaster building, it scared the hell out of Ansely. "Holy fuck!" Had echoed across the towering bleached buildings.

The metropolis of Sharronn was hushed and empty. That kind of stillness only I was accustomed to. A storm of 'fucks' reverberated across streets and down each row of pristine, white buildings. Les, Judas, and I jumped simultaneously as the crevasse in the Philex wall continued to widen.

"I'm sorry, I know I should be accustomed to the strange." Ansley was relaxing under Les' confused gaze. "I just… I don't know what I was expecting."

"Oh," Les turned from Ansely to the now completed opening and said, "Yes, the closing function in the arena and ship are turned off."

We had moved past the idea of an off switch as soon as the crowd of colorful Par began to form. If I had been standing on the roof of the capitol the scene would have resembled bacteria populating the floor of a giant's mouth and we were about to walk onto the tip of the behemoth's tongue. We made our way to the exit and the wall began to open for us. We were met with the same stunning silence as when we entered the street. It was as if the Par were in a vacuum or a projection instead of living, breathing creatures. My years of solitude had not prepared me for this kind of crowd, and I could tell the rest of my crew were equally disturbed. As we stepped around the side of the stage and made our way to stand behind Whitt the crowd remained silent, but the anticipation hung like humidity in the air.

"Hello, Par of Sharronn. Please, join me in welcoming your new Kara warrior squad."

I did not know how Whitt was projecting her voice across the large plaza, but her soft soprano had suddenly become a booming baritone that was soon joined with the cheers of the thousands of Par stretched as far as my eyes could see. The large courtyard forked into many side streets, also lined with buildings.

A thunderous echo vibrated my skull. I looked up to see portals opening along the sides of each building and I could see lines of Par beating the Philex rhythmically.

"Now," with one word from Whitt the audience was silent once more. "As you are aware, these are the humans that our Leap squad came into contact with only a few cycles ago. They are from a galaxy so far away that they were not affected by the anti-Kara that was inflicted upon us by the Vokkna nineteen rotations ago."

She paused for dramatic emphasis and motioned for me to step forward. I shifted awkwardly as Les nudged me toward her open hand as she said, "And this is Elinor."

I felt as if the entire crowd had taken a step forward. Whitt continued, "The female that has not only become the strongest Kara warrior of her squad but has also been the first human to breed with a Par, thus creating yet another Par hybrid that will continue to project the Par species across both space and time."

The masses erupted. I could feel their desire to know me. Know my thoughts and fears, my past and future, and all I wanted to do was drag their hopes for me in the dirt. I wanted to disappoint them and turn their joy into pain. They did not care about me or my squad; they only wanted progress for their own species, whatever it took. Whether it was through peace with the Vokkna or by using us to destroy them, as long as their species thrived, they did not worry about the cost.

As my mind raced with thoughts of loathing for the population, I would soon risk my life to save, Whitt had continued to talk of plans for war and the desecration of the entire Vokkna species, and eventual domination of their planet. The Par hung on every word. I had expected riots and cries for peace from Sharronn, but soon saw that it was not a sense of compassion for the Vokkna the drove them to peace, but the fear that they would not win. Now that they were assured that the Kara infected humans would in fact fight for them, they were more supportive of the war than ever.

I did not want to fight for the Par anymore; I wanted to kill them myself. The beating on the portals pounded in my ears and their tribal chant filled my mind, but I could not understand the meaning of the phrase the masses called out to me, and then everything went black.

"Elinor, are you in pain?" Les was lightly shaking me and the chanting had stopped. "Elinor, please you must tell me what is wrong, or I cannot help you,"

"Well, obviously she was freaked out. We all were, right?" Bo asked as woke to find myselve once more in the lobby of the capitol. I later discovered that I had froze as Whit attempted to ask my thoughts on my upcoming motherhood, when the chanting started.

"What were they chanting?" Odelia whispered. "The whole thing was so… militant."

"The phrase didn't translate?" Shurr asked. "The chant is an ancient Par war cry. It refers to the giving of life and the taking of life, and how both are equally important."

"It was a basic war rally." Tikk cocked his head at Kang. "This is not how humans prepare their masses for war?"

"No," Kang shook his head. "That was scary. I mean, people got over excited at stuff like that; Kepler's last uprising is a perfect example, but we are never that organized and… quiet. The silence was the scariest part, and what Whitt did our there... the control over the crowd she had... I've only seen that kind of control on historical videos of Earth."

"The chanting stuff hit home." Alva added. "I remember seeing quite a bit of chanting in videos of the 20th and 21st centuries."

"So, that's the norm?" Kang asked Tikk.

Les had moved away to talk to Whitt as she entered the room. Stillness had once again fallen over the mass of Par and I could see them slowly dispersing. I watched an average sized male Par, the color of dying leaves, his eyes alive with a passion, make his way from the front row to join in the line of Par streaming into the opening on the side of the building to our right. The hole in the Philex had grown to full capacity, reaching the windows that had flanked the wall, allowing filing clerks, negotiators, administrators, and janitors back into their place of work.

There were new taxes to process and businesses to demand voluntary donations from. Ad campaigns to be organized and set into place and food to be imported. We had scared them with our strangeness at first, but my quiet freak out had won their hearts. Whitt was ecstatic with the outcome of my timidness, and she was pouncing on the opportunity to Paranize us. We had a power that all of them coveted but none of them could acquire, but we were small and attractive in our obscurity, so they accepted us. I had shown the Par that we were just as scared and unprepared as they were, and despite my ability to kill all of them, in that moment I was a female that was in no way prepared to care for the life that was growing inside of her. I was weak like them, and the Par, like most creatures, enjoyed seeing weakness in animals not themselves.

Whitt's voice broke my train of thought. She had been saying something I am sure she would remember as profound, but I had forgotten to pay attention. I caught the last part. "Until then, please get rest and continue being the shinning beam of hope you are, Elinor, I am truly inspired by you. Do not let the masses get to you. They are not what is important here, you are."

"Thank you." I was taken back by Whitt's squeak of joy and Les' hand tightening around my waist until I realized this was the first thing I had said since being pulled out of the rally.

"Can we go home?" I was over all of it. I turned my head into Les' chest and gulped down his scent.

"Yes, of course." I suffered Les' arms as transport back to the cargo ship that had just appeared in the now vacant plaza. The portals along the buildings were gone once more, which allowed us to exit in privacy. I had never envied the administrative life, but the life of the average working Par at this time was a dismal reality to think of.

"That was anticlimactic." Judas shrugged as we made the quick leap into the cargo hold of the arena. "Did you guys do that just so we would appreciate training more, because I have zero interest in doing another one of those spooky mind control shows again."

"You're just mad that nobody paid any attention to you." Ansely replied as we exited the ship. I remained in Les' arms. More than willing to go wherever his aroma took me.

"Well, Elinor's freeze got all of us off the hook for another cycle at least." Ming took hold of my foot as it dangled in front of her and squeezed. I flexed my toes around her fingers, and we held appendages for a few paces.

"I am sure we are all hungry, and a bit disgruntled as well, but that will not excuse anyone from missing Kara training this evening. We will have plenty of time to eat and get in a few hours before last meal." Shurr said to a response of groans. "You just declared your new-found appreciation for training." Shurr shoved Judas which was returned by a running shoulder nudge.

"I might appreciate a day off every once in a while." Judas said as the wind was knocked out of him by Shurr's large form.

"I suppose if you do not wish for me to teach you my throwing technique--"

"Fuck you!" Judas aimed his shoulder at Shurr again but missed and stumbled into the hallway wall. "You've been putting that off all week and now it's time, come on." Judas turned sharply into the arena and Shurr caught his shoulder.

"Perhaps some sustenance first, you will need your strength."

That evening, I found myself hovering above the new Philex mat while Ming did the same on the opposite side. We spoke loudly without caring who heard us. "So, do something next time instead of just standing there like an idiot," she called to me wavering in the air as her bright blue Kara shifted from the back of her left arm to her shoulder.

"I don't know what happened. I was ready for a rally full of protestors that would back up my point, but instead they just listened to what she had to say and blindly cheered whenever there was a long enough pause. I don't know what would have happened if I had declared my disdain for the war and urged everyone to spend their money on communicating with the Vokkna rather than exterminating them."

I pushed myself closer to the sky and pressed my olfactory memory to recall the essence of Les after a long run.

"I don't think it would have gone too bad. That crowd would do whatever Whitt told them to do, and she legitimately seems to like you, or she really is amazing at her job," Ming said.

"I believe it is the latter. Anyone related to Grymm has to be full of shit." We both laughed and I shifted to hover on my stomach. "I'm coming to you," I said, and Ming imitated my position.

"Go for it," She said as I shifted a portion of my Kara concentration to the bottom of my feet and I began to drift towards Ming. I closed the gap as I silently gazed into my friend's almond eyes. I finished the journey across the mat in her arms and we lowered to the floor. The embrace had been added only a couple turns ago. It required us to turn off the Kara supply to our arms and balance while our lower body produced, and then read each other's speed and movements so we landed simultaneously.

"Yurrlu?" She asked with her face pressed into the soft mat.

“Yes," I said as I slid to the ground.

Les and Urral were in the dining room when we entered and Ming's face lit up when she saw the pink male.

"Where have you been?" She said snaking her arm around Urral as I poured both of us a jar of Yurrlu.

"I took the day to visit Hurran. Oolang had requested a medical visit a couple turns ago and I thought today would be good since the arena would be empty.”

“But if you had gone on a different day, I could have joined you." I had stopped drinking my Yurrlu mid gulp and nearly spilled on myself during my angry outburst.

"Yes, Oolang did mention your desire to revisit, but... I," a sideways glance from Urral towards Les was all indication I needed.

"Are you seriously trying to keep me from going to Hurran? What do you think will happen?" I shifted my scowl to the purple brute and filled the room with tension.

"Elinor, please..." Les raised his hand only to have it slapped by me.

"We are talking about this. Your room. Now." I chugged the rest of my Yurrlu and stomped down the hall. I could hear Les following me and turned into his room quickly so I could be waiting for him. I did not want to talk. I was too angry to speak to him, and if he made any attempt at justifying his actions, I knew I would kill him.

As he turned the corner, I used his speed to my advantage. I pulled his heavy body towards my own and we collapsed on his bed. He had not expected physical contact and quickly thrust himself upward onto his hands and knees, straddling me.

"Is this what you want?" His voice was calm, but his features quivered with the effort of suppressing emotion, and his voice was agonized. I soaked in the power I had over him.

"Yes, but I still want to fight." I slapped him across his nose and his extra nostrils flared as he took hold of my wrist and pressed himself down to cover my soft skin with his rough flesh.

“Good," He whispered as he pulled my top and shorts down towards my ankles. I slipped out of my Philex and helped him do the same, and then I pounced on his large form. Swinging my fists at his beautiful jaw line as I settled on top of him. Les never swung back at me, but he always defended himself. This time he wrapped my arms around my back and gripped me in an unbreakable embrace. I was forced to kick and lunge with my legs, which worked to my advantage.

Once again, I owned him.

I knew it was his DNA inside of me that was causing

my visceral reaction to him, but I didn't care. I wanted him, and I could feel his compulsion for me. I thrived on his need.

I beat him as I rode his body. I found pleasure in causing him pain. I convulsed as I slapped his chest and face again and again. I now know he derived as much pleasure from my abuse as I gained in giving it. The only way I was ever truly able to hurt Les was to deprive him of my pleasure. Les came when I came. I could see the elation in his black eyes as he basked in the joy exuding from my blue ones. At times I would look away as I came or hide my face in a blanket, forcing down my cries of elation. I would keep my pleasure from him. Those were the times when I was a truly selfish lover.

28.

I awoke the next morning to the realization that my current urge to be far away from Les was nearly as strong as my urge for him to be inside of me the night before. I decided somewhere off planet was the best place for me at that current conjuncture.

I slid out of his enveloping grasp and searched for my Philex.

"Again, you grow weary of me so quickly." I lifted my gaze from my Philex shorts to meet his judgment. "We are connected now Elinor. You will need to accept your desire for me sooner or later. The need will only grow when the child is born."

I was not comforted by his seemingly forced intimacy.

"I want to go to Hurran, as per our agreement, I have every right to visit when it does not affect training."

I had my clothes collected and was walking toward the exit.

"But you have training today." He sat up and cradled his knees.

"I can go after and return tomorrow before morning cardio; I see little problem with me missing lecture. I will not be allowed to take part in the attack during the peace summit either way."

I did not wait for his answer. I was across the hall in the cleansing beam before he could speak again.

I ran with a vengeance that morning. Judas was not able to keep pace and every time he came upon me doing a strength interval, he puffed out a complaint.

"What the fuck, El? Are you mad at me?" He threw himself down where I was transitioning between angled position and board position. My abs were burning, and I had no desire to calm down yet, but he deserved a reason for my sudden push.

"I was with Les last night," I said without looking at him, but I could feel his eyes burning into my cheek.

"You're not going to be able to hold onto those sympathy points if you keep fucking the guy." He had caught his breath and joined me in an angled position.

I collapsed and contemplated my next statement. "I never wanted sympathy," I said as I pressed myself up to standing. "I would prefer my actions to remain unanalyzed." I ran from his answer and was on a ship for Hurran before he made it back to the arena.

***

I was greeted by Oolang as I stepped off the cargo ship, "I am pleased to see you, Elinor."

The mechanical voice that emitted from the translator did not do the illustrious visual language justice. I answered in Vokknan with a sweeping of my arms, a loud stomping of my feet, because I could not make the booming sounds the Vokkna created by grinding their trillions of limbs together and finishing with a flip of my head to imitate a Vokkna vertical sand burst.

"Your Vokkna is coming along quite well. I can tell you have been practicing with the tutorials I sent you." Oolang lead me through the caverns of Hurran.

"I will never be completely fluent due to my lack of limbs and solid form," I giggled as Oolang flashed white and dark blue.

"The effort is and will be appreciated. I have been in discussion with the Vokkna leaders and the summit is set for one lunation from now. Where do the Par stand?" We entered the small chamber that held Trrcck, who began to stir.

"If anything, they are only more prepared for war than ever before." I attempted to use both Parian and Vokknan simultaneously for Trrcck's sake, but I only knew enough to translate a portion of what I said. "We had our first propaganda rally and have three more scheduled before the summit."

The room echoed with the sound of grinding rocks as Trrcck settled itself in a position to observe our conversation. Trrcck had become just as fascinated with my language as I was with its.

"The Par are terrifying in mass, and don't seem to think for themselves. They ate up everything Whitt said. I have both Les and Grymmig's word that they will listen to what the Vokkna have to say before launching an attack, but I fear their promises are empty."

The Vokkna burst into action and I struggled to understand its quick movements.

Oolang translated and attempted to calm Trrcck as it began to smash against the sides of the Phiex sphere, "Trrcck is obviously upset. It knows that this means death for many of its kind. The Vokkna have no real defense against the Kara. That is why their main goal was blocking the Par's ability to use it. Now that you are here… you have changed everything."

Trrcck shifted and I sought to find a connection with this astonishing creature, and I believe it was attempting to do the same.

I had been practicing a specific dialogue for the past few turns, and I endeavored to communicate it with my limited assets. *I do not want to fight you. I desire peace. The Par leaders will fight you because they are selfish and want your resources. They have told me it is your species that wishes to fight because you believe you are superior to all others based on the truths you hold sacred within your culture. Is this so?* I settled my arms at my sides and waited for a response.

It was Oolang who spoke first. "Your language is incredibly adept for a beginner with very limited movement, Elinor."

"Thank you. I have been practicing." I smiled at Oolang then returned my attention to the swirling matter formation that loomed before me.

The Vokkna shifted uneasily under my gaze before it began. *The Par speak the truth. I was taught from a small age to see all those that do not know Kvvgjtt created life for their sacrifice as inferior. I was taught that Par only demand sacrifice, but I now know the truth and have informed my leaders of my communications with the Harlukkna, and my leaders are prepared to discuss peace, but I believe their true intentions are similar to the Par."* With help from Oolang I was able to comprehend Trcck's speech.

Have you informed your leaders of me and the other humans, and our ability to harbor the Kara? I asked.

"We have not allowed Trcck to communicate without supervision. The Vokkna are unaware of your existence." Oolang answered.

"But you still believe they will come to the peace summit prepared to fight?" I focused my attention on Trcck.

I know they will. They see the Par as weakened; they will make the first strike.

"It is exactly what Grymm wants. If the Vokkna strike the Par will feel every right to counter attack, and the war will be reborn," I said to Oolang.

But you can choose not to fight. Trrcck pleaded with us. I could see the desperation in its quick movements. *The Kara warriors are the only advantage the Par have. If you refuse to fight. There will be no war.*

"It is not my call. I will not even be on the floor during the summit, and I know my fellow warriors will not back down when attacked. They have been preparing for this for the past eight moon cycles, the Par saved us from ourselves. We owe them our lives. It appears there is very little any of us can do." I said, looking from Oolang to Trrcck and then silence.

The air was filled once more with the crunching of rock as Trrcck compressed into a solid form; our conversation was over. I pressed myself against the Philex bubble and said, "I must return to Qualittia, but I will see you again before the summit.

Why, if we can do nothing to change our fate? Trrcck's movements were angry now.

"I don't know. Because I would like to speak with you more. I won't visit you if you do not want me to." I was saddened by my inability to help the creature and even more disheartened by the fact that I was the cause of its disillusionment.

No, I would like to communicate. I have never known a species other than my own, and it is comforting to know there is compassion in the universe.

Oolang had to translate most of this for me and then I had to leave quickly after because my tears made both of them uncomfortable.

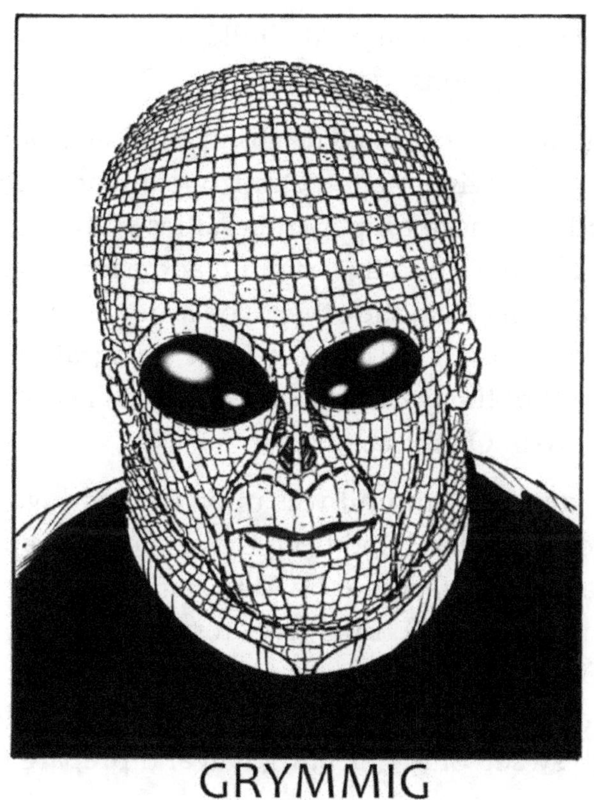

GRYMMIG

29.

I was true to my word and visited Trrcck and Oolang two more times before the summit. I was continuously amazed by how similar our three cultures were. We all had strong family-based societies that depended on a hierarchical system. We all saw education as the key to progress, and we all longed to live our lives without interference from outside antagonisms. Our differences melted into the background as we discussed our passions for storytelling and shared the folklore that shaped our separate civilizations.

Ming had begged to come along, but Les would not approve her leaving planet. Our troop attended an image shoot and two more propaganda rallies within the lunation leading up to the summit, and each one was more unsettling than the other. The ardor for war could be seen throughout the cities as large holograms of me and the rest of the warriors were projected across the architecture of Qualittia.

The day of the summit was upon us, and I was no more prepared than I had been the first day I stepped on Qualittia, and the fact that I had to stand aside while the rest of my crew risked their lives for a cause I did not support only made my dread deeper. We arrived on Hurran a turn before the summit in order to conduct a thorough sweep of the meeting hall and prepare for the worst.

I had not informed Les of the Vokkna's plans to attack in hope they would change their mind. With or without my input the Par where fully prepared to do battle and had no expectations of an actual discussion. Grymmig was on site within a fraction of our landing, and he oozed confidence as he pranced around the tunnels of Hurran shouting orders at anyone in his general vicinity.

"Elinor, this is where Les and you will observe the summit. You will be able to see the action clearly without the danger of being seen or dragged into the battle. We do not want you and your little bump in any peril." Grymmig smiled at the lump projecting from my abdomen. I could feel my Kara shift and wriggle, but I suppressed the urge to destroy the annoying male; his time would come.

"Is it a one-way portal?" I asked as I looked down on the expansive hall far below us.

"Yes, anyone looking up will see a rock surface identical to all the others." Grymmig explained. "A creation of the Harlukkna, not anti-Kara, but there was no need for it to be when it was created. You will be safe, and Les has explicit instructions on how to get off planet if things escalate."

Les had remained uncharacteristically quiet during our exchange. I turned to him and asked, "Do we know how many Vokkna will be attending?"

"Oolang has informed me that thirty life forms should arrive within the next five fractions, but at least half of those are lower level combatants. We will likely have their eight leaders and officers attend the summit while the others remain on the landing dock." He replied in a monotone manner. Les had grown more distant with every visit I made to Trrcck.

"Does each Vokkna have an individual ship?" I asked.

"In a way," Les replied with a confused smile. "They become part of their ships. They must carry a part of their home planet with them in order to travel and survive. They are an extremely resilient life form, but not without limitations." He smiled to himself.

"I assume they are able to detect our essences just the way we are able to detect theirs," I said.

"Your body heat will throw off their censors. They will know there is an unidentifiable existence on planet, but they will not know what it is." Grymmig answered this time.

"What about the Kara? Will their ships not detect that?" I turned between the two as I asked.

"The Kara was destroyed before the Vokkna were able to perfect that technology, and all Kara detection was dismantled over ten rotations ago." With this Grymmig broke into one of the creepiest, quietest laughs I have ever heard. My innards tightened at the thought of his joy.

"How long do we have?" I avoided Grymmig's eyes while moving near the exit.

"The summit will officially begin in half a turn. You may join the rest of the squad in the holding chamber until then." Grymmig gave his permission.

Les walked with me and Grymmig trailed behind, but close enough to keep me looking over my shoulder in case he decided to touch me.

The squad was buzzing with energy as they chugged Yurrlu and paced the small holding chamber outside the main meeting hall. Judas lunged toward me when I entered and asked, "El, you hungry?" He tossed his empty container to Lyttl, which was refilled and handed back to him.

I paused too long and found a jug of Yurrlu in my hands before I spoke. "A little out of it?" Ming asked.

"I'm not even doing anything. You all seem so calm." I looked around the room at my comrades.

"I think it's easier for us." Alva spoke up from the corner where she was sitting. "I'd be freaking if I had to just sit back and watch after nine cycles of buildup."

"But maybe nothing will happen." Ming chimed in with optimism. "The Vokkna could surprise us."

"The only ones getting a surprise will be the Vokkna." Bo said and he and Luke bumped forearms in the traditional Kara warrior manner. They were so excited I could not bear to bring my doubts into the blithe atmosphere.

"This is not the time for celebration." I was thankful for Les' solemn statement. "We must focus. Judas, lead the group in strategy breakdown." Judas surpassed me as a leader.

"Troop formation!" He led his crew in a quick tactical practice as Les and I looked on.

"We will adjust the formation accordingly when the Vokkna arrive, but the basics are strong." Shurr spoke up as I watched my friends prepare for a fight, I longed to take part in.

"They will not even have a chance to complete their initial strike before we have infiltrated the hall and wiped them out," Shurr continued.

He had such confidence I could not help but feel our

victory was eminent. My thoughts shifted to Trrcck, who was now free of his Philex prison, and waiting in the large meeting hall for his fellow Vokkna to arrive. He was our bargaining tool and bait rolled into one. I feared the reproach of my comrades more than I wanted to save him, and for that I will forever be ashamed.

"Do not fret; you will take part in many great battles." Les whispered in my ear.

"You misinterpret me. I would be completely satisfied if I was never given a chance to use the weapon you put inside of me." I was angry, but unlike what I thought at the time, it was not Les who caused my aggravation.

"Perhaps it would be best if you and Elinor rested in the viewing room." Shurr said as he unloaded Philex mats for the crew. "We all need to maintain our strength and focus." He looked at me with disapproval.

"Shurr is right." Les said as he pressed the small of my back.

"I get it." I raised my hands in submission. "Let me at least say goodbye to them." I moved toward Judas as he reabsorbed his Kara ball. "I love you, please be safe." I said as he wrapped his arms around me.

"We got this, El." He said as Ming, Alva, and Bo joined in to make a wall of warmth.

"Do you have your device," Ming asked as we disengaged. "Take some videos of us so we can watch how badass we are later." I laughed at the absurdity of the idea but promised I would do as she asked.

"I don't know what to say, I just want you all to be ok, promise me that much, please." I asked as I pulled the device out.

"We'll all be ok, El." Judas spoke for the group and I really believed him. "Now get out of here so we can make some kind of attempt at sleep."

Les and I returned to the small room overlooking the meeting hall. He had brought mats for us and we lay beside each other without touching for a few moments, but I could not resist the warmth from his body. I rested my head on his chest.

"You are scared for your comrades," he said as he cradled me. No response was needed. Neither of us slept but we rested in each other's embrace until the Vokkna's arrival was announced.

30.

I leapt to my feet as soon as I heard movement, and Les joined me when we heard Oolang's voice announce the arrival of the Vokkna and the beginning of the summit.

The portal blocked us from the view of those below, but I could hear everything clearly. The entering ceremony was very formal with the Harlukkna and Par standing at attention when the Vokkna entered. I had not been prepared for how gigantic the Vokkna leaders would be. Trrcck was a tiny flurry in proportion to his commanders. The sound of colliding rocks reverberated around the hall as the Vokkna settled themselves into solid form. I was amazed that no one was hit by a rogue Vokkna limb, but the Vokkna clearly had more control over their whirling forms than it appeared from the outside. Oolang began the summit by introducing those present.

"We welcome the Vokkna representatives." The majority of Vokkna names are comprised of movement, with only one or two sounds to accompany them, and so the eight Vokkna became known to me as short bursts of consonants. Vrrk, Gfft, Nddf, Rqqx, Prrm, Hjjk, Urrt, and Ltth were the representatives from Vokkna.

“The Par are represented by,” Oolang continued, “Grymmignactla 5354, Whittmignactla 95667, and Shurrantyluk 78865. I, Oolang, will act as translator and facilitator."

"Enough with formalities," Grymmig said stepping forward. "What are the Vokkna's intentions?"

Oolang translated and with a screech and a burst of brown particles the Vokkna responded violently. Trrcck appeared to be cowering behind them. Shurr made the quick motion that indicated his order that the troop ready themselves. I could sense Judas on the peripheral.

"The Vokkna demand..." Oolang paused and had a moment with the Vokkna. It was clear that Oolang did not approve of their demands, and their movements where so quick and sharp that I could only make out bits of what was being said. Oolang eventually submitted to their loud injections. "The Vokkna require a complete submission of the Par in order to come to a peace agreement. The Par will hand over all planetary ownership to the Vokkna and will only be allowed to remain on Qualittia or Tralcaccia as laborers."

"This is obviously not agreeable." Grymmig appeared extremely satisfied as he stated this. "And what action will the Vokkna take if we refuse their offer?" Les' hand rested on my back as we held our breath.

All eight Vokkna leaders whirled in place, and raised themselves to their full height with a rumbling echo. I pressed myself against the cold portal surface in anticipation of my Kara warrior's entrance.

"The Vokkna will eliminate the Par, thus removing the need for approval of these demands," Oolang said and stepped back with a motion of submission and sympathy. "There is no need for this. A different arrangement can be made, or trade can continue as is."

"The Vokkna have made their demands known." Grymmig beamed at his statement. "If they are unwilling to negotiate a more hospitable agreement then our only solution is to finally finish this war."

My crew burst forth in full battle mode, and the eight towering leaders where whipped away in a rainbow of engulfing mist, but they were soon confronted by the Vokkna's backup, who had also been waiting at the ready. Oolang appeared beside me as the fight cascade across my field of vision. The gigantic chamber was alive with a kalidascope of color and the cacophony of crashing stone. I could not make out who was where, as my comrades were lost in a mass of churning Vokkna particles. My jaw pulsed and Les' grip on me tightened. I pressed myself harder against the screen separating me from my family.

Suddenly, a massive flash of Judas' white Kara shot across the room and five Vokkna were consumed before my eyes. The burst of bodies made it possible for me to make out Judas in the mass of soaring stones. He ran towards Trrcck who was still cowering in the corner and began to release another ball of Kara but then turned to retreat instead; he was depleted.

I panicked as I watched Trrck and Judas realize their situation at the same time. My breath escaped my lungs as Trrcck sailed through the air and consumed my brother.

"Judas!" The portal I had been leaning against was

gone before I even made the decision to join the battle.

"Elinor, no…" Les' words rushed past me as I jumped into the open air.

As most people experiencing shock, I do not clearly remember the moments that followed my flight from the portal. All I remember is the gut-wrenching pain that pulsed through my body as I made my way toward the place I wanted my brother to be. My vision was filled with gritty Vokkna; my body came crashing down on top of Trrcck and the creature that had become my friend was gone in a green haze.

The man that had once been my favorite person in the entire universe disintegrated onto my chest. Judas was now just ashes smearing my skin black. I no longer wanted peace. I wanted death and destruction, to extinguish every one of the Vokkna and watch them slowly disappear under my fingertips. They would not have time to feel my pain, but I didn't care; I wanted to ensure I never saw a living Vokkna again. I would kill everything they held dear and then wallow in their extinction.

Again, I do not know exactly what I did to bring about the total annihilation of every Vokkna on Hurran. All I know is that I willed it; I desired their obliteration and I gave all of myself to make that wish come true. I would have given more. I would have gladly died that day with my brother, but I suppose my life was not necessary to accomplish the task.

My Kara escaped my pores and dissolved every

Vokkna within range, all without a second thought from me. The mist swept across the remaining Vokkna warriors, but somehow did not pierce the skin of my allies, and before I was aware of what happened the Vokkna were gone, with only my ashen skin to remind us of what had just occurred.

"Elinor…" I gazed up to find a melancholy Les. Sadness suited his features and I allowed Ming to guide me to my feet. I wanted to blame him, wanted to blame Grymmig who could be seen scanning the room from the far corner, but I was drained of my fervor and all that was left was a vacant space. I accepted Les' amaranthine embrace as he said, "I believe I am forming an emotional attachment to you Elinor."

I felt warm liquid seeping down my inner thigh, and everything went black.

End Volume I.

www.ingramcontent.com/pod-product-compliance
Lightning Source LLC
Chambersburg PA
CBHW071543110726
47908CB00007B/1980

* 9 7 8 0 9 6 5 7 1 1 3 7 1 *